GW00367282

IND<u>E</u>X
ON CENSORSHIP

INDEX ON CENSORSHIP 2 2001

WEBSITE NEWS UPDATED WEEKLY

www.indexoncensorship.org
contact@indexoncensorship.org
tel: 020 7278 2313
fax: 020 7278 1878

Volume 30 No 2 March/April 2001 Issue 199

Index on Censorship (ISSN 0306-4220) is published bi-monthly by a non-profit-making company: Writers & Scholars International Ltd, Lancaster House, 33 Islington High Street, London N1 9LH. *Index on Censorship* is associated with Writers & Scholars Educational Trust, registered charity number 325003

Periodicals postage: (US subscribers only) paid at Newark, New Jersey. Postmaster: send US address changes to *Index on Censorship* c/o Mercury Airfreight International Ltd Inc., 365 Blair Road, Avenel, NJ 07001, USA
© This selection Writers & Scholars International Ltd, London 1999
© Contributors to this issue, except where otherwise indicated

Subscriptions (6 issues per annum)

Individuals: Britain £39, US $52, rest of world £45

Institutions: Britain £44, US $80, rest of world £50

Speak to Tony Callaghan on 020 7278 2313
or email tony@indexoncensorship.org

EDITORIAL

Bush fires

The year has opened to ordered anarchy. Since our last issue, the ungovernable forces of nature have contended to outdo the more calculated malevolence of humanity.

In India, Salvador and Mozambique, TV screens recorded the death and flight of tens of thousands of victims from earthquake and flood; in Afghanistan, up to 1,000,000 'internally displaced' wander the countryside or queue at frontiers, seeking escape from the drought-ridden desolation of a country already laid waste by over 20 years of war.

We didn't see the Afghans on our screens; nor will the aid we watched arrive in Africa and India reach them. The West has turned its back on the last great proxy battleground of the Cold War, abandoning it first to the mercies of warring *mujahedin* it had created to fight our war against the USSR and, when that failed, turning it over to a bunch of religious zealots in the hope of 'strong' government, the protection of US interests and not too many questions asked.

But the Taliban have slipped the leash. Not only can they no longer guarantee the all-important pipeline that will bring oil from Central Asia to a friendly haven in military-ruled Pakistan, they have plunged Afghanistan into a silence so profound that even music, dancing and the flutter of pigeons' wings are banned. As is kite-flying, TV and videos. Veiled women, forcibly condemned to ignorance and total subjection to their menfolk, creep around, invisible in the shadows. And now, for the second time, totalitarian mullahs threaten an act of cultural genocide in retaliation for UN sanctions against Afghanistan: to bomb to extinction the unique and extraordinary Buddhist statues in the Bamiyan valley. 'Only' statues: symbols, perhaps, of the millions of dead and disappeared in the course of Afghanistan's wars – and the hungry ghosts waiting at borders.

Shortly before this, the US and UK had indulged in a little bombing expedition of their own. As in Afghanistan, the complex politics of oil have more to do with February's assault on Iraq than allegations of Iraqi attacks on UN aircraft. Saddam is a monster, bomb him away. And place the people who have suffered his butchery since 1968 in double jeopardy.

But the 1,000 or so Iraqi Kurds who, not surprisingly, chose this moment to flee the tyranny of Saddam and the bombs of their protectors, found little welcome among the latter. Anti-immigration rhetoric is gaining ground, intolerance raises its head above the ramparts of fortress Europe.

Meanwhile: the rump IRA tried a little censorship by bombing against the BBC and, in Israel, Sharon rules. Nothing moves in Gaza; Palestinians throw stones; Israelis shoot to kill. ❏

contents

Greek gods
& monsters
p141

KEEP EUROPE NEANDERTHAL!!!

Martin Rowson
opens his regular
slot with a go at
Europe
p56

Index awards

On 5 February, *Index* held the first of what will become an annual awards ceremony. It was a chance to honour those who take great personal risks in the defence of free speech, and to remind us that, for many, freedom of expression comes at a heavy price. The event was hosted by Jon Snow and introduced by Harold Pinter.

Most courageous defence of free expression

Mashallah Shamsolvaezin
Editor-in-chief of Iranian newspaper *Neshat*, Shamsolvaezin was jailed in April 2000 for publishing an article critical of capital punishment, and has since been placed in solitary confinement. Over the past two years, Shamsolvaezin's paper has been banned four times: *Neshat* is its latest incarnation.

International whistleblower of the year

Grigory Pasko
A journalist and former naval officer, Pasko was responsible for revealing that Russian military vessels were secretly dumping radioactive waste in the Sea of Japan. After breaking the story in November 1997, Pasko was incarcerated in a military prison, where he was detained without trial for two years.

Best circumvention of censorship

Publius Censorship Resistant Publishing System
Devised by Laurie Cranor, Avi Rubin and Marc Waldman, Publius is an online encryption service that has been successfully used by human rights organisations to evade government censors.

Award for services to censorship

Ministry of Defence (MOD)
Using the threat of prosecution under the Official Secrets Act, the MOD has made it virtually impossible for 'whistleblowers' to expose malpractice within the military and intelligence services. Nigel Wylde, Tony Geraghty and David Shayler are among those to have fallen foul of its draconian rules in recent years.

Index would like to thank the following for supporting the event: Axis and One Aldwych, Harold Pinter, Jon Snow, Michael Grade, Geoffrey Hosking, Ian Nicolas, Candace Allen, Jocelyn Burton, Lisa Forrell, Norman Jewison, Patricia Finch and Sir Simon Rattle

*From **Harold Pinter**'s introductory speech*

" Censorship comes in many shapes and sizes: it can be trivial, silly and even pathetic, but it can also be arbitrary, brutal, elaborate, complex, far-reaching and very dangerous. I'd like to give an example of a sustained, elaborate and really systematic form of censorship. It happens all along the line, but I want to quote a particular case.

In November 1989, the year the Berlin Wall fell and everybody said how wonderful it was that millions of people had found freedom, six of the most distinguished Jesuits in the world were murdered in cold blood at the University of Central America in El Salvador. Their cook and her daughter were also killed – shot in their beds. Their assassins were members of the elite Atlacatal battalion, trained by US special forces at Fort Bragg in North Carolina.

There was one witness to this atrocity: a housekeeper who saw the murders from her window. She hid for the rest of the night and, in the morning, informed the Jesuit provincial. She was taken to the French embassy, where she delivered her testimony. French diplomats then took her to the airport to fly her to safety, but the US ambassador intervened and insisted that his officials take her to Miami. She was met there by the FBI, taken to a hotel and held incommunicado for four days. She was interrogated, not only by the FBI, but also by a high-ranking Salvadorian army officer. She was told that she was a liar and that it was known she had sexual relations with the Jesuits. When she was finally released, she said that she had seen nothing at the university – no soldiers and no murders. The US ambassador declared that, in his view, FMLN guerrillas were responsible. He said that they had probably stolen army uniforms and pretended to be soldiers. However, one year later, nine soldiers did go on trial. Seven were acquitted, even though two of them had actually confessed. Two were convicted and sentenced to 30 years in prison. A presidential amnesty released them after 18 months.

There are a number of questions to do with this matter that have never been answered. Who were the intellectual orphans of these murders? How far did knowledge and responsibility extend? The truth has been effectively censored and suffocated by an elaborate tapestry of deception, obstruction, manipulation and lies. The truth has been buried alive – it has never been told. What we do know is that the guilty walked free and that they were, and are, in all sorts of very high places: the Salvadorian government and military hierarchy, the US state department and, of course, our old friends the CIA.

Index's role, which it has sustained admirably over so many years, is to excavate the real facts and expose the truth. *Index* bears witness with total objectivity, but with proper indignation. Long may it continue. ❑ "

[In October 2000 it was announced that the investigation into the murder of the Jesuits would be reopened. Ed]

news in the

● **Calendar cover-up** A photograph of a priest, naked except for a 'dog collar' and a Bible to cover his 'sacraments', was removed from a charity calendar in January following a complaint from the Most Reverend James McLoughlin, Bishop of Galway. Father Olan Rynn had agreed to strip off for *Bare Shakers 2001*, a fund-raising calendar for cancer sufferers.

● **Revolutionary reruns** To ensure people fully celebrate the 80th anniversary of the founding of the Chinese Communist Party on 1 July, the government has ordered all soaps and dramas to be pulled from TV schedules in June and July. The schedules will instead be graced by such offerings as *Sun rises in the East* and a series called *War to resist US aggression and aid Korea*.

● **Transparency rules** The UN Transitional Administration in East Timor has issued a directive reminding its employees, most of them East Timorese, that they are forbidden to speak to anyone, anywhere, ever about the mission's activities on the island, unless they first obtain written permission, which will probably be denied.

● **Toy story** Raging against 'the monsters [that] have caused physical and mental damage to young people', Mexico City pastor Father Ramon Hernandez implored children in February to bring their dolls, magazines and video cassettes and throw them on to a blazing pyre. The ritual burning was the climax to a day of exorcisms of things that 'contain subliminal messages that dispose children to evil'.

● **Can't pay? Daren't pay!** Thousands of Russian churchgoers are refusing to pay taxes after Orthodox priests declared that the barcodes on their returns were stamped with the mark of the Beast. Theologians say that three lines at the beginning, middle and end of the barcodes, when translated into decimal, add up to 666, the mark of the Antichrist. Priests have urged congregations not to fill in the forms lest they hasten the apocalypse.

● **Untitled** The Tate Modern show 'Century City' displays a surprising timidity in view of the 'cutting-edge' gallery's recent dalliance with the British school of shock art. A recent exhibition of Soviet posters provides translations of all their titles except one above a picture depicting a row of identical black circus performers dressed in penguin suits. The curators may have felt that art-lovers, having swallowed Tracey Emin's soiled underwear last year, probably wouldn't stomach the concept, 'Chocolate Boys at the Leningrad Circus'.

● **Academic arabesque** An Egyptian student was expelled from Cairo's American University in early January for wearing a black veil to class. University officials claimed that the woman represented a 'security threat' and would be impossible to teach. Farouk El-Hitami, vice-president of the university, said: 'No teacher wants to speak to a veil. There are lots of considerations when someone wants to masquerade like this.'

● **Crowd control** Weeks of anti-Japanese propaganda in the run-up to the Nanjing massacre anniversary whipped up such a mood of fury among citizens that police ended the day battling in the streets with more than 10,000 protestors, and news agencies were banned from reporting the incident. And after rumours spread that Nanjing's Sheng Dao Grand Restaurant had named its VIP suite after the Japanese emperor (it hadn't), the crowd turned demonic, trashing the joint to the sound of anti-Japanese slogans.

● **Police bullying** A 16-year-old Canadian boy was slung in jail in mid-December for reading aloud a story he had written as a homework assignment. The student had suffered from repeated bullying and wrote a fantasy, called 'Twisted', in which he described himself wreaking bloody revenge on his tormentors. The police were summoned and the boy taken away for questioning. He was finally freed – but more than a month later – after a galaxy of writers, including Booker Prize winner Margaret Atwood, campaigned for his release.

● **Battle lines** New Hampshire officials were in uproar in early January after a newly elected Republican representative proclaimed that all police officers should be killed. Calls for Tom Alciere's resignation flooded in after he commented: 'Nobody will be safe until the last cop is dead.' Alciere, who had law-making powers in the state congress, also lauded convicted cop-killer Carl

Drega, who shot two state troopers in 1997, as 'an innocent man taking out enemy troops in battle'.

● **Trial by ordeal** A student from Broken Arrow, Oklahoma, was suspended from high school in January for practising 'witchcraft'. When her ceramics teacher was rushed into hospital with stomach pains, assistant headmaster Charlie Bushyhead accused 15-year-old Brandi Blackbear of casting a spell over him, and banished her from the campus. It transpired that the teacher was suffering appendicitis, but Blackbear received no apology. On the contrary, teachers raided her locker, only to discover a pentacle sketched on a piece of paper. Blackbear is now appealing against her exclusion, a process that requires her to prove that she is not a witch.

● **Celestial scapegoats** Muslims torched bars and hotels in the northern Nigerian city of Maiduguri in reaction to January's lunar eclipse. Local religious leaders claimed the 'supernatural' event was triggered by sinners, prompting youths to unleash a wave of violence against houses of debauchery. One participant was quoted as saying: 'The immoral acts committed in these places are responsible for this eclipse.' Police fought with gangs of Muslims until sunrise, when the crowds melted away with the dawn.

● **Warning: earth moving** Not content with seismology, Indians have been looking for other causes of January's terrible earthquake in Gujarat. A minister in the province of Karnataka, T John, told a World Peace Day conference that the earthquake was caused by a wrathful God 'venting his fury' on Gujaratis for their destruction of churches and ill-treatment of religious minorities. Meanwhile, hundreds of Muslims ceremoniously hurled televisions from the rooftops of Surat and Ahmadabad after a cleric blamed the earthquake on 'immoral broadcasts'.

● **Trade descriptions sex act** A sex shop owner in York was fined £6,000 in mid-January for selling videos that were 'too tame'. Voyeurs who paid Nick Griffin's Little Amsterdam up to £50 for a copy of *Confessions of a Sex Maniac* were treated to the harmless story of an architect seeking to build an office block fashioned on a pair of breasts. Those who bought *Secrets of a Sensuous Nurse* endured a 30-year-old comedy starring Ursula Andress and Jack Palance. Prosecutor Michael Taylor said: 'These films can be seen on television . . . they were certainly not the most interesting of videos.'

• **Eavesdropping in Skopje** A scandal, dubbed the 'Macedonian Watergate', erupted in January when it was revealed that the phones of up to 100 opposition figures, including 25 journalists, had been bugged. The incident was brought to light by the country's largest opposition party, the Social Democratic Union of Macedonia (SDSM). At a press conference held on 17 January, SDSM leader Branko Crvenkovski revealed he had evidence implicating the government and police in the eavesdropping episode, accusations that Defence Minister Ljuben Paunovski denied.

According to Crvenkovski, wire-tapping began in September 2000 when the ruling coalition of President Boris Trajkovski came perilously close to defeat in local elections. Crvenkovski claims that the VMRO-DPMNE government could only have clung to power by monitoring and spying on the opposition. He also alleged that over 1,400 pages of private conversations between reporters and opposition activists had been transcribed.

Among the journalists who faced surveillance were the editor of *Dnevnik*, the producer of Sky Net TV news and Julijana Kocovska-Krtolica, a correspondent for the daily paper *Denes*. Said Kocovska-Krtolica, 'this is a sign that our rulers have become so paranoid they are scared of anything that resembles democracy'.

Countering claims in the daily *Skopje* that the government has the capacity to bug 2,000 people, the interior ministry contended that phone-tapping on such a scale was simply not possible given the police's lack of resources and equipment. Under pressure from the European Parliament, Prime Minister Ljubcho Georgievski has ordered an inquiry, though the opposition holds little hope that it will topple the government: Stavre Dzikov, the state prosecutor leading the inquiry, is a government appointee.

Paul Hoffman & David Gelber

• **Lighten our burden** The Association of Serbian Journalists (ASJ) has launched what it describes as a 'moral purge' of its members in an attempt to rid the profession of those who loyally served ousted leader Slobodan Milosevic. In an attempt to salvage something of its tarnished reputation, the organisation has begun to expel the editors, reporters and directors who spent years 'misinforming and deceiving the public, in contravention of the journalist's ethics'.

The process resembles the Prague lustrations of 1991 during which public bodies were systematically cleansed of communist functionaries and collaborators. Following the Czech example, the ASJ has called a series of public hearings to establish the responsibility of those accused of using the media to disseminate propaganda. Milorad Komrakov, editor-in-chief of Radio Television Serbia's current affairs division under Milosevic, was the first to face expulsion from the ASJ after the organisation's disciplinary committee found him guilty of 'subordinating professional journalism practice to the narrow interest of the country's former political management'. Others facing dismissal include Djordje Martic, editor of *Politika Ekspes*, Zivorad Djordjenic, director of the daily *Borba*, and Dragan Antic, chief-executive of the Tanjug news agency.

The ASJ's decision to banish members who abetted Milosevic has aroused considerable enmity among several journalists. Many have refused to attend the hearings while others, fearing that corruption charges will be levelled against them, have fled the country. Slavisa Petrovic, former editor of *Bor Smelter* magazine, was not just speaking for himself when he recently described the ASJ and the country's democratic forces as 'scum, fifth columnists, quislings and foreign mercenaries'. But such comments have been parried by the ASJ. Miroslav Turudic, a senior committee member of the organisation, described the purge as an opportunity to encourage a new generation of journalists to join an association 'which did not carry the burden of the past'.

PH & DG

● **Kuwait's custodial freedom**
'Kuwait is free,' announced returning Gulf War 'hero' and new US Secretary of State Colin Powell in Kuwait on 25 February. He was celebrating the enclave's decade of freedom from Iraqi occupation – but not that of its people. Women's liberation and democracy remain off the hero's agenda. Just nine days before Powell joined the unelected Kuwaiti ruler, the Emir Sheikh Jaber al-Sabah, to commemorate the country's liberation, the Constitutional Court rejected without explanation a submission for voting rights for women.

Also unexplained was the banning of over 300 books from the 25th Kuwaiti Book Fair. 'We didn't even ask for a reason – we knew it would be useless,' said the director of one Arab publishing house, adding that 40 of her 200 books were deemed unacceptable. 'Some publishers were close to pulling out but, having already paid for flights and hotels, chose to cut their losses by staying. Next year may be different.'

This year the censors set up an office inside the fair. Matters were complicated by the presence of not one but three censors, each sent by different ministries. They didn't always see eye to eye.

Books touching on religious issues, politics and women's rights were all banned. Other authors, including Mohammed Arkoun and Hamed Shoukri, appear to have been blacklisted. Meanwhile, author Laila al-'Othmann, who had earlier fallen foul of publishing laws which prohibit criticism of the Emir, the economy and Islam (*Index* 6/1999), was stripped, on the eve of the fair, of an award she had won a fortnight before for her book, *Yehedeth kul Leila* (He Talks every Night). Kuwaiti literary associations said the move 'sucked their hopes dry'.

'Particularly when you think of all the self-censorship which goes on beforehand,' said a spokesman for a publisher in London, 'it's all a bit of a farce really.'

Neil Sammonds

• **Chinese Nobel** Gao Xingjian, the first Chinese writer ever to win the Nobel Prize for Literature, made his first visit to his homeland in January since collecting the award late last year. Xingjian has lived in exile in Paris since the authorities declared him persona non grata in 1989 after he condemned the Tiananmen Square massacre.

Sixty-one-year-old Xingjian has long been a critic of China's communist regime. As far back as 1986 his play *The Other Shore* was banned on the grounds that it was subversive. Since then, none of his works has been published in the country. Xingjian used his Nobel Prize acceptance speech to lambast the Chinese censors. He claimed that the Communist Party had nearly 'wiped out' literature during the Cultural Revolution, and said that dissident writers still faced being 'crushed' under the present leadership of President Jiang Zemin.

Beijing officials declined an invitation to attend Xingjian's talks. A spokesman for the foreign ministry denounced his speech as a 'vicious attack, ignoring the facts', while the *Yangcheng Evening News* commented, 'it's ludicrous that such an awful writer should win the Nobel Prize for Literature . . . the Swedish Academy has made a big joke of the Chinese'. Xingjian retorted by commending Taiwan, over which China has never relinquished its claims, as a beacon of freedom in an ocean of oppression.

Ben Carrdus

JUDITH VIDAL-HALL

Stop press

In Chechnya

'Thou shalt not get into a strange vehicle; thou shalt not be alone;
on the sixth day, thou shalt always disappear from the hotspot you
are visiting'—*Anna Politkovskaia, Commandments for a Russian journalist*

Anna Politkovskaia, a journalist with the weekly *Novaya Gazeta*,
has been writing about what she refers to as the 'humiliated and
oppressed' – 'those driven to despair and deprived of home, family,
health and any hope for the future' – in the territories of the former
Soviet Union since the 1980s. In autumn 1999, she turned her attention
to Russia's second Chechen war. After reading her outspoken reports
from the Caucasus, the Russian authorities withdrew her accreditation.
Since then, she has continued to visit the region at great personal risk,
reporting not only on the state of the Chechen population, the razing
of Grozny, a city that 'makes Sarajevo at the height of the Yugoslav war
look like a picnic', but also on the corruption at the top of Russian
military command that has abandoned and brutalised troops in the field.

At the end of February, she travelled deep into the war zone to
investigate complaints of 'constant hunger, unbearable cold, total
isolation from the outside world, lack of medical care and, in particular,
about brutal punitive raids on their villages by the federal forces stationed
on the outskirts of the village of Khottuni' that had been sent from the
region to *Novaya Gazeta*. Several hundred people were asking to be
helped to move out of Chechnya to any place in Russia as soon as
possible.

Any doubts she may have had about facts 'as fantastic as they were
glaring' were abruptly cut short when she herself was detained and
abused by Russian troops on 20 February. She describes what happened
in *Novaya Gazeta*:

Anna Politkovskaia

'Your papers are false, you are one of them [the Chechen rebels],'
I was told. Then followed interrogations for hours on end. I
omit the disgusting details of the interrogations because they
were utterly obscene. But it is these details – and my tormentors
couldn't have imagined it – that provided the key proof that
everything the Chechens had earlier told me about tortures and
manhandling was true. . . . The nightmare ended with a flight
out of Chechnya . . . back to Moscow. On the way back, all the
isolated stories I had heard, all the episodes of my trip, clicked
into one whole. That's when I drew the final conclusion . . .
All this is happening in our country, here, now. Under the
existing constitution. Under a 'strong-willed' president who is
its guarantor. . . . With human rights activists, both government
and independent, working to ensure people's rights. . . . And
still, despite all that, there are the pits, the 'children's mittens',
the 'dancing' [forms of torture described by AP in the article. Ed]
. . . and nobody will dare to say that I have not seen it or heard it
or touched it. I have experienced it myself.

The Russian authorities have denied all her claims, accusing her of
lying and 'fantasising'.

'Retired'

13 December 2000: Massoud Behnoud, in prison garb, conducts his own defence

On 1 March, the Iranian courts announced their verdict on freelance journalist and film-maker Massoud Behnoud, first arrested on 13 December last year. Despite a number of trumped-up charges including the use of drugs and alcohol, and 'spying' for the BBC, his main offence, as with the many journalists currently inhabiting Iran's jails (see p35), was simply to have told it like it is, in print, for all to read. He conducted his own defence and, in the face of great pressure to 'repent', instead proffered his 'retirement' from journalism. It did not save him from a 19-month sentence, but it does, effectively, silence one more journalist (*Index* 5/1999 'Fifth time lucky?'). He had until 21 March to appeal.

Stand-off

After denouncing the violence and 'false democracy' of President Yoweri Museveni's March elections, Major Okwir Rabwoni, head of the youth section of presidential rival Kizza Besigye, was forcibly arrested at Uganda's Entebbe airport after a five-hour armed stand-off on 20 February. He was released the next day and left soon after for the UK. ❑

JVH

Okwir Rabwoni: arrest at Entebbe airport.
Credit: Cranimer Mugerwa / New Vision

JIM D'ENTREMONT

Poison from the proletariat

Fierce critic of the dark side of US society, or vicious, foul-mouthed wizard of hate? White rapper Eminem, the music industry's hottest property and sworn enemy of 'concerned parents' everywhere, is in trouble – but not with his teenage fans and followers

That's why the city is filled with a bunch of fuckin idiots still (still)
That's why the first motherfucker poppin some shit he gets killed (killed)
That's why we don't call it Detroit, we call it Amityville ('Ville)
You can get capped after just havin a cavity filled (filled)
Ahahahaha, that's why we're crowned the murder capital still (still)
This ain't Detroit, this is motherfuckin Hamburger Hill! (Hill!)
We don't do drivebys, we park in front of houses and shoot
and when the police come we fuckin shoot it out with them too!
That's the mentality here (here) that's the reality here (here)
Did I just hear somebody say they wanna challenge me here?? (huh?)
While I'm holdin' a pistol with this many calibres here?? (here??)
Got some registration and just made this shit valid this year? (year?)
Cause once I snap I can't be held accountable for my acts
and that's when accidents happen,
when a thousand bullets come at your house
and collapse the foundation around and they found you
and your family in it (AHHHHH!)

'Amityville', *Marshall Mathers LP*

'You think I give a damn about a Grammy?' sings Marshall Bruce Mathers III, the 28-year-old white rapper who performs under the name Eminem. Michael Greene, president of the National Academy of Recording Arts and Sciences (NARAS), which confers the American music industry's most prestigious honour, has reciprocally called Eminem's *Marshall Mathers LP* 'the most repugnant album of the year'. But in January 2001, the membership of NARAS nominated the record for four Grammys – including the award for Album of the Year, repugnant or otherwise. The subsequent uproar may have cost Eminem the top prize at the 43rd annual Grammy presentation on 21 February, but he won in three other categories, including Best Rap Album.

Outside the Los Angeles arena where the ceremony took place, protests against NARAS' recognition of Eminem were led by the Gay and Lesbian Alliance Against Defamation (GLAAD), the National Organization of Women (NOW) and the Family Violence Prevention Fund. About 200 demonstrators distributed leaflets tracing alleged links between Eminem's 'hate speech' and violence, waved placards denouncing bigotry, and read statements condemning both the controversial rapper and openly gay British pop star Sir Elton John, who joined Eminem in performing the song 'Stan' at the event.

Eminem's records, emblazoned with parental warning labels in the US, include tracks entitled 'Kill You' and 'Just Don't Give a Fuck'. In 'Kim', which Mathers calls 'a love song', he escalates a fantasised domestic argument into an emotional apocalypse ending in his wife's murder. In some songs, he consciously gay-baits: 'My words are like a dagger with a jagged edge that'll stab you in the head whether you're a fag or lez,' he asserts. 'Hate fags? The answer's yes.'

'Eminem's lyrics do more than glorify violence against lesbians, gay men, transgendered people and women,' GLAAD's Joan Garry told the press. 'They also give permission for young people to abuse and harass people who are "different", numbing them to the damaging impact of homophobia and misogyny.'

While GLAAD stops short of demanding outright censorship of such lyrics, some gay and feminist leaders have been less cautious. 'The producers and promoters of the record . . . need to consider the ramifications of these lyrics and pull the product off the shelves,' Jeffrey Montgomery of the Triangle Foundation, a gay rights organisation in

Detroit, Eminem's home town, told reporters soon after the May 2000 release of the phenomenally popular *Marshall Mathers LP*.

The record's international success has elicited censorious responses around the world. Ontario Attorney General Jim Flaherty recently tried to have Marshall Mathers himself barred from Canada. In New Zealand, where chief censor Bill Hastings pronounced Eminem's songs 'sugar-coated poison', record retailers face three months in prison and a NZ$10,000 (US$4500) fine for selling an Eminem album to anyone under 18.

In the UK, the suicide of 17-year-old Eminem fan David Hurcombe sparked concerns that some virulent form of nihilism absorbed from Eminem's music caused the young man's death. The students' union at Sheffield University banned the music from campus radio, forbade the student newspaper to review Eminem's records or concerts, and proscribed the wearing of Eminem T-shirts. The National Union of Students and the British gay activist group OutRage! picketed Eminem's sold-out February concerts in Manchester and London; OutRage! sought to have the singer 'disinvited' from a scheduled appearance at the London club Ministry of Sound.

The ire is directed at a singer whom Elton John has called the most important voice in popular music since Bob Dylan, and whom *Newsweek* magazine has described as 'the most compelling figure in all of pop music'. A nimble satirist, Eminem writes with wit and passion. The

Eminem: who gives a damn?
Credit: Andrew Hobbs / Camera Press

rage he vents is tempered with a savage humour that spares no one and is frequently directed at himself. His most recent North American concert series was aptly named the Anger Management Tour.

A protégé of Dr Dre, an artist turned producer whose rap group NWA (Niggaz With Attitude) provoked international moral panic in the early 1990s, Eminem, a white practitioner of an art form steeped in black culture, is no more confrontational, homophobic or sexist than many equally compelling black rappers – none of whom, with the possible exception of Ice T in his 'Cop Killer' phase, has been subjected to such militant opposition. Endowed with a rhyming facility that places him in a direct line of descent from the late Tupac Shakur, Eminem enjoys a greater degree of success with black fans than any other white rap artist (*Index* 6/1998: *Smashed Hits*). He is widely, though not universally, respected by the predominantly black hip-hop community. The sensibility he shares with black rappers encompasses a class awareness that cuts across race. The rage and despair of the underclass is the lifeblood of rap.

In the US, Eminem's most strident critics belong to the affluent left and the secular right. Blue-collar leftists, who have little use for the decidedly upscale gay and feminist movements, share many of Eminem's working-class social concerns. Religious reactionaries, who find his lyrics free of Marilyn Manson-style blasphemies demanding redress, have no problem with Eminem's apparent homophobia.

Rich US conservatives and their corporate liberal allies have a Pecksniffian disdain for members of the lower orders who pursue what US culture teaches them to want: money and power. The only form of humanity they find more distasteful than a defiant working-class brat is one who achieves financial independence. With refreshing candour, Charles Murray of the American Enterprise Institute cites Eminem in a 6 February *Wall Street Journal* column as a symptom of the process of 'proletarianization' that is tearing civilisation asunder.

Subverting the myth of American classlessness, Eminem exposes the delusions of a society that resolutely denies its own failings and inequities. The social class that produced Eminem is all too aware that the United States, a place where prosperity is largely for the already prosperous, is a nation that deals with overlapping problems of race and poverty by punitively defunding social services, building more prisons and stepping up its use of the death penalty.

Speaking as Slim Shady, his dark alter ego, Eminem tells hard truths about a violent culture. In 'Amityville' he paints an unflattering portrait of industrially blighted, crime-ridden Detroit. In 'If I Had', he describes the lot of millions of young Americans working dead-end jobs for below-subsistence pay.

'Eminem's songs reflect a conversation that goes on among young people all over America,' observes Nina Crowley of the Massachusetts Music Industry Coalition. That conversation slices through official pieties and upper-middle-class cant, and advocates, in unexpected ways, personal and parental responsibility. 'When a dude's gettin' bullied and shoots up his school/And they blame it on Marilyn [Manson] . . . and the heroin/Where were the parents at?' Eminem asks in 'The Way I Am'. His depiction of drugs, though infused with humour and a streetwise knowledge of their allure, is relentlessly negative.

For every troubled teenager like the late David Hurcombe, there are thousands of young fans who feel empowered by Eminem's messages. 'His lyrics make me laugh and think at the same time,' says 19-year-old Clint Sumner, who is in a non-abusive relationship with the mother of his four-month-old child (named Hailie Jade after Eminem's daughter), and who is proudly devoted to his gay older brother. 'Some of his lyrics are offensive, but people need to realise it's just music,' Sumner insists.

'I'm a criminal,' Eminem complains, 'cause every time I write a rhyme, these people think it's a crime / To tell 'em what's on my mind.' The prevailing, comforting myth is that the music is at fault, not the culture. It is always easier to suppress a song than to confront the social reality it expresses. ❏

Jim D'Entremont, an arts journalist and playwright, is head of the Boston Coalition for Freedom of Expression

RAY FURLONG

Soft as velvet

**Neither Prague nor, remarkably, Brussels seems in a hurry
to guarantee media independence in the Czech Republic,
one of the darlings of EU expansion**

The sight of thousands of people on the streets of Prague last
Christmas demanding an end to political meddling in public
television raised the question of just how far press freedom has advanced
in eastern Europe over the last decade. The answer is that although the
stone-faced newsreaders of communist days have gone, politicians still
have an unhealthy degree of influence.

The crisis at Czech Television (CT) erupted when Jiri Hodac,
formerly of the BBC Czech Section, was made head on 20 December
last year – less than a week after his predecessor was sacked. Believing
the appointment to be politically motivated, staff reacted by interrupting
the main evening news with the statement that it was impossible to
choose a new director-general so quickly. The message ended with
the words: 'The last independent television station is under threat!'

Things deteriorated in the days that followed. Rebel journalists –
backed by a motley coalition of artists, actors, singers, celebrities,
writers and intellectuals – occupied the CT newsroom, from where they
broadcast bulletins stating their case. President Vaclav Havel supported
them. The new management reacted by deploying security guards outside
the newsroom, who allowed journalists to go out, but not back in again.
Thousands joined nightly protests outside the building. Food and drink
were hoisted in through the windows on a makeshift pulley – as were
portable toilets for Hodac's security denied access to the office facilities.

The drama was played out on television screens across the country
as the two sides vied for control of broadcasting. 'Rebel' newscasts
were cut off, to be replaced with bulletins made by a hastily assembled
team loyal to Hodac. These 'official' news programmes were crudely
one-sided, reminding many of the news Czechs were served under

Czech TV, December 2000: civic triumph over the establishment.
Credit: Rene Volfik / CTK / Camera Press

communism. At one point Hodac switched off all broadcasts for 23 hours. In the end he stepped down citing health reasons, after 100,000 people massed on Wenceslas Square calling for his removal – and for an end to political manipulation of public television.

The numbers were swollen by general political frustration, particularly with the Civic Democratic Party (ODS) of former prime minister Vaclav Klaus. Many voters, especially in Prague, feel betrayed by Klaus because he agreed to prop up a minority Social Democrat government in 1998 – after an election campaign in which he pledged to 'save' Czechs from the 'dangers of the left'. Klaus said the struggle at CT was not about freedom of speech, but a simple political battle from which his rivals – President Havel and the so-called Four Coalition (4C) of small opposition parties – sought to gain political capital. He pointed out that prominent 4C politicians joined the protests from the start, even camping out in the rebel-held newsroom.

Klaus's ODS was the only party to back Hodac to the hilt, and Hodac's own political sympathies are well known. At one time he had been talked about as a possible ODS party spokesman. Also worrying

to insiders at CT was his appointment of Jana Bobosikova, a former
economic adviser to Klaus, as head of news: she. During a stormy
parliamentary debate on the crisis, one 4C deputy described the
appointment of Hodac as 'a Yuletide putsch' – to which Klaus banged
his fist on the table in anger.

Protesting journalists also pointed to Hodac's time as head of news
at CT for a few months last year when he had proved dangerously
pliable. There was the case in which Hodac sacked a leading anchorman,
Roman Prorok, the day after he hosted a debate with Klaus and current
Prime Minister Milos Zeman. Both politicians had phoned CT to
complain about how the debate was handled.

Hodac has now gone, a new head has been appointed and the
protests have stopped. But the heart of the problem is the political
composition of the CT Board of Governors, and this remains an
unresolved issue. Last spring, the Board was replaced with new
governors appointed on a party-political basis: four for the ruling
Social Democrats, three for the ODS, and two for the 4C. It was a
media coup which attracted very little attention at the time.

Jan Jirak, head of the Board from 1997–2000, recently wrote: 'The
CT Board, which is supposed to be the only supervisory organ carrying
out the public's right to supervise, became a de facto executive body –
the wishes of the lower house of parliament.' Given that the Social
Democrats and ODS dominate the lower house, there is plenty of room
for suspicion of political interference. There is also some proof. When
the Board started looking for a new head of CT, the leadership
of the Social Democrats openly held meetings to discuss who should
get the job.

The ODS was more subtle, but its media specialist Ivan Langer –
who is also head of parliament's media committee – was in constant
contact with the head of the Board, Miroslav Mares. A leaked copy
of Mares's mobile phone bill showed he had phoned Langer 138 times
in December, while Social Democrat MP Miroslav Kucera was called
130 times by a governor nominated by his party, Jiri Kratochvil. These
cosy ties were long-standing, but it seems there were attempts at direct
censorship. Former CT boss Dusan Chmelicek, whose sacking made
way for Hodac last December, told public hearings subsequently held
by the upper house of parliament that Langer had earlier called Mares to
complain about two current affairs programmes. Mares had then called

on him to have analyses of them drawn up, examining the complaints.

The situation in other former communist central European states, which are similarly front-runners for admission to the European Union, is sometimes worse than in the Czech Republic. Polish television (TVP) is headed by Robert Kwiatkowski, who masterminded President Aleksander Kwasniewski's victorious election campaign in 1996. In Hungary, the opposition Free Democrat party is now proposing a law to change the system under which political parties appoint people to media regulatory councils.

'After the events in Prague it is impossible to ignore that the system of councils run by political parties has failed. Media, paid for by taxpayers, have also become dependent on the government in Hungary, and become an old-fashioned tool for propaganda,' said party spokesman Miklos Haraszti, a former dissident. Of course, the last ten years have also seen the emergence of a network of private TV stations across the region but, even here, politicians control the strings through their systems of allocating licences.

The Czech TV battle showed people were willing to fight for politically independent media, but this was not much of a victory. The new broadcasting law passed by the Czech parliament following the sit-in at CT actually increases political control, while the Board of Governors is still appointed by the lower house of parliament, leaving plenty of scope for interference in the future. The idea that appointments to the Board could be made by other institutions – the Church, trade unions or other interest groups – was not even discussed. The new law also gives the lower house powers to sack individual governors – and the entire Board – at any moment it chooses for 'not fulfilling its public service function', whatever that means at the time. The conditions under which the Board can sack the director-general are equally vague.

The EU's expansion criteria stress candidate states must have stable democratic institutions in order to join the new European family. The Czech Republic may be a leading candidate for membership, but there is clearly very little interest – either in Prague or in Brussels – in creating a more robust system of checks and balances to minimise political influence in the public media. ❏

Ray Furlong *is a BBC stringer in Prague*

VLADIMIR GUSINSKY

Waiting game

Russian media tycoon Vladimir Gusinsky, under house arrest in Sotogrande in Spain since 12 December, says he would be prepared to sell a substantial slice of his holding in NTV, Russia's only independent national television network, provided he has 'a 100 per cent guarantee that it will remain independent and that the Kremlin will stop putting pressure on its journalists'.

Gusinsky is waiting for a decision on the Russian public prosecutor's request for extradition. The prosecutor's office accuses him of fraud for allegedly paying his debts of US$180m to the state-owned Russian company Gazprom – a 46 per cent shareholder in NTV – with assets illegally salted away abroad. Gusinsky, however, claims he is the victim of a police operation to silence criticisms of the Kremlin by his Media Most group, the most significant independent press, radio and TV group in Russia. NTV has been outspoken in its criticism of the government and army's conduct of the war in Chechnya. Many in Russia believe this is a part of President Vladimir Putin's attempt to bring the media back under government control (see also p16).

Gusinsky made his announcement shortly after the meeting between representatives of US press magnate Ted Turner and Gazprom in Moscow on 5 February. He spoke to Almudena Martínez-Fornés in Sotogrande on 19 February.

Would you be prepared to sell part of your shares to Ted Turner or another foreign investor?

The Russian authorities – the Russian president – do not like me because I take an independent, critical line. If the personal price I have to pay for the independence of my television network is to sell the majority of my shares to independent investors, then, as long as they guarantee 100 per cent that they will never make an agreement with the Kremlin which would put the independence of NTV in doubt or allow intervention, then so be it. For me it is not a question of money but of principle.

This is important to me: what's happening at NTV has nothing to do with money, but with the thousands of employees working for the company. I need to be sure that the journalists are not going to be put under pressure.

I'd be happy if Gazprom really were welcoming foreign investors. But Gazprom is not on its own in this; it's a government tool. I hope it's an honest proposal and they are not saying one thing now so they can do

Vladimir Gusinsky.
Credit: European Press Agency

another later. It's obviously not good for the president of Russia, with all his talk of democracy, to be seen to say, 'I'll ease the pressure if you sell your business.' That is not democratic; it would be unthinkable for Chirac in France or Bush in the USA, for instance.

Even if this deal goes ahead, you're still waiting for the extradition request to be resolved one way or another. What do you think will happen?

How can I say: the decision lies with the judges. But let me explain the difference between justice and injustice: under an unjust system, court decisions are anybody's guess; under a just one, it's not a matter of guesswork. I hope they don't succeed in turning a business matter into a criminal transaction.

But I'm not the only one in this situation; there are many others. This battle began a while ago and the best evidence that this case is political is the agreement signed in July last year when Putin and the prosecutors sent me to jail in Moscow, saying they would only free me on condition I sold my share of Gazprom. How much more do you need to prove my case is political?

Yet many people might regard your fortune with suspicion. How can you accumulate so much wealth in a few years without breaking the law?

First of all, it has been more than just a few years; I'm not so young any more. It's taken 12 years. Second, we have built up not only the largest media group in Russia but also one of the largest in Europe, and when you do business you tend to make money. We have television channels, radio stations, newspapers, magazines, and we are the best across the entire spectrum. Our radio station offers the best news bulletin in Russia, NTV can be seen in Europe, Australia, the US, Canada, Israel, the Middle East. Russian speakers can watch NTV all over the world. Here in Europe it has three channels.

They say that many years ago you worked as a taxi driver and theatre director?

I did both. It's no secret, but it's a long story. If I'd been in the US, I could have talked about the great American Dream. I was born into a family with troubles: my grandfather died in a concentration camp in 1937 when Stalin killed many prisoners. My grandmother spent eight years in a concentration camp as the wife of an 'enemy of the people'. And, for seven years, my mother and her twin sister could not live in Moscow as, under Soviet law, the children of 'enemies of the people' were not allowed to reside in the capital. My family has a complex history; and it wasn't rich.

I studied in the navy for two years and then went to college. I married and my first son was born while I was still a student; I needed money to support my family. That was why I drove a taxi. At the start of *perestroika*, I organised one of the first co-operatives in Russia. They were the basic units of production, the smallest and the simplest.

Do you believe Putin is deceiving the West when he talks about democracy? Isn't he really a dictator?

Not exactly. It's more complicated. In its 1,000-year history, Russia has never known democracy. Anyone who ventures into the Russian countryside now will see no difference between the totalitarian and a non-totalitarian regime. What happened in the ten years that preceded Putin was unique in the experience of Russians. Over ten years, people were being slowly injected with democracy. We hoped it would be enough, but it didn't take on everyone. As a result, many Russians who know only the old system don't understand what freedom is or the price that must be paid for it.

They want their safe little salary and their safe little job; they want to be able to go to the shop and buy cheap vodka whenever they want. That much, at least, had been guaranteed by the old regime for 75 years. Putin represents a new phase of that order. I'm not saying Russia is returning to communism; communism belongs in the past. But Putin represents the authority of the past, with its panoply of security services – the KGB, the armed forces, nuclear weapons – teaching its neighbours to respect its power, rather than a normal life, normal wages, a strong economy and good state productivity. It's a big problem, for the country – and for its neighbours. ❏

Translated by Catherine Forrest from an interview in ABC, *February 2001*

T J CHENG

Horizon from Taiwan

Media boss Jimmy Lai Chee-ying wants the world to know that he didn't leave Hong Kong because he was forced out – by the powers in Beijing or by anyone else

L ai made his fortune in the clothing business in the 1980s, but it was as a magazine owner that he became famous. In a 1995 editorial in his flagship weekly tabloid *Next*, he called the then premier Li Peng among the worst of Chinese insults – a 'turtle's egg' – for his role in the Tiananmen Square killings. For his insolence, Lai was forced by other shareholders to sell out of Giordano, the clothing retailer he founded and made a success across Asia. Undaunted, he started Hong Kong's first tabloid newspaper, *Apple Daily*, which dished out homicides and sex scandals, while heaping criticism on the mainland authorities, urging them towards political reform. Lai's publications are still banned in China.

These days Lai's eyes are on Taiwan, where he is setting up the operation of his Hong Kong-based Next Media Group. Lai moved his family to Taiwan last year after the opposition Democratic Progressive Party (DPP) won the presidential elections last March, ousting the Kuomintang (KMT) after more than 50 years of rule. The KMT, which relocated to Taiwan after losing the civil war to the communists in 1949, had built a prosperous Taiwan, but prosperity was the KMT's eventual undoing. As Taiwan became more middle class, its voters became more independent-minded. Since the end of martial law in 1987, the island has developed its own raucous style of democracy as opposition politicians began to dismantle the KMT's ironclad control of the electorate. With the DPP's victory last year, Taiwan became the first democracy in Chinese history, thereby challenging Beijing's assertion that Chinese people are not 'suited' to democratic values.

Taiwan's media need a jump start. Credit: © Chris Stowers / Panos Pictures

'Being Chinese, we're all excited about the first democracy in China,' Lai says of Taiwan. 'The temptation to live here was so great.' In May, he plans to launch the Taiwan edition of *Next* and is confident that the magazine's style will win a large audience in a population of 23 million. 'It's no different from Hong Kong when I first launched *Next*,' says Lai. 'Definitely this market needs something fresh.'

Lai thinks Taiwan's influence on China will come to replace Hong Kong, which is steadily being marginalised as it pulls closer into the Chinese sphere of influence. Since the handover in 1997, politicians in Hong Kong have learned to kowtow to Beijing, while Taiwanese politicians continue to challenge it. 'It's not the leaders of China who will be influenced,' says Lai, 'it's the people. Mainland Chinese will soon come to see Taiwan as a role model for solving their own problems and, when that happens, can the leaders resist? No way. Very simply, Taiwan is the most dangerous totem in inducing China's future democracy.'

The 'one country, two systems' approach, installed as a compromise following the 1984 Sino-British talks over the future of Hong Kong, is constantly being eroded. The fact that, despite his lack of popular support, Chief Executive Tung Chee Hwa is assured of a second term in office is a case in point. The recent resignation of the capable bureaucrat and Tung rival, Chief Secretary Anson Chan, is another sign of Hong Kong's gradual demise as a 'free' entity within the Chinese orbit. Recent efforts by Hong Kong politicians to bar the persecuted Falun Gong from practising in the Special Administrative Region are another.

'Hong Kong is slipping from the world stage,' concludes Lai. 'Will Hong Kong still be prosperous? Will it still be a free port? I say yes. But will Hong Kong still have a great influence on China? Yes, but to a far lesser extent than Taiwan. Hong Kong was instrumental in China's opening but the next stage has to be in the political arena, and Hong Kong has no way of setting an example in that direction. Taiwan is the natural catalyst.'

Lai insists that he didn't leave Hong Kong because he was forced out. People have speculated that a recent business defeat at the hands of Hong Kong's pre-eminent tycoon, Li Ka-shing, may have been the spur that sent him packing. Lai's *Next* magazine has published scathing reports on Li's monopolistic control of the Hong Kong economy and the tycoon's strong links with Beijing. Lai's now defunct Admart, an online supermarket business, openly challenged Li's Park 'n Shop supermarket chain until Lai shut it down late last year, having been being bled of nearly US$100m during a two-year period after a bloody tit-for-tat battle against Li's online businesses.

'If I was not scared away by the Communist Party,' Lai says of the rumours, 'I would hardly be scared away by Li Ka-shing. With due respect, I would not like to have Li Ka-shing as an enemy, like, but he was not the reason I moved here. Nor was Beijing. I came to help build the future of China.' He believes that China will be a democratic state within ten years and that Taiwan will be the launch pad for his own eventual assault on the mainland media market. 'In the not too distant future,' Lai concludes, 'China will be a Taiwan, a very, very big Taiwan.' ❏

T J Cheng is the senior correspondent for Greater China at Asiaweek

FRED HALLIDAY

Revolution at the crossroads

The next few months may be decisive for the future direction of Iran and for the fate of the revolutionary regime. They could also seal the fate of the many journalists and writers languishing in Tehran's jails

An air of uncertainty and anxiety hangs over Tehran, now a smog-laden city of 12 million. No one, Iranian or foreigner, is confident of how the next few months will turn out, of whether the reformist current that has swept the country since 1997 will continue, or will founder, or be overturned, in the face of determined and possibly violent conservative opposition.

The presidential elections of 1997, in which Mohammad Khatami triumphed as a reform candidate, and the *majlis* (parliamentary) elections of February 2000, appeared to confirm that a strong majority for reform exists. But these messages from below are met by a ruling elite that is divided, and part of which is alarmed by the calls for change. The next testing point will be the presidential elections scheduled for June 2001: nothing, not even President Khatami's commitment to running for a second term, is as yet certain. A revolution that in 1979 swept all before it now faces difficult choices, both abroad and at home.

The pressures for political and social change in Iran are accompanied by widespread debates about the direction of the country, about the further development of the revolution, and about Islam and the modern world. Nothing could be more inaccurate with regard to the discussion in Iran, and its relation to the outside world, than a simple contrasting of 'Iranian' or 'Islamic' values, and ideas, with 'western' ones: there is as much diversity within Iran, and within Islamic discussion, including within the clergy, as there is in the international East–West dimension. For those of a secular orientation, the influence of Marxism, prevalent two decades ago, has now yielded to an interest in liberal thinking: Popper and Mill, not to mention theories of 'civil society' and a 'third way', have replaced Lenin and Mao. There are those in Iran who want to keep the system established by Ayatollah Khomeini in the revolution and the eight-year war with Iraq: there are many who believe it should change, and some who wish it could remain the same but realise, and fear, that if it does not change it will be swept aside. The fate of the Shah, and that of Gorbachev, are very much in the minds of the Iranian political elite.

The dramatic elections of recent years have nonetheless altered the political climate in Iran. There is a strong movement for change, a movement that is named after the Persian date on which Khatami was elected, the Dovvom-i Khordad (2 Khordad or 17 May 1997). Part of this protest comes from above: it is expressed by Khatami in his call for the rule of law and civil society. But more important, there is clamour for change from below.

The issue that has provoked most controversy in recent years is that of freedom of expression. The Ministry of Islamic Guidance administers censorship but book publishing is relatively free in Iran, provided core issues pertaining to religion and the state are not touched. You can buy a whole range of books on modern Iranian history. Frank McCourt's *Angela's Ashes* has sold well in Persian translation, a success not unrelated to its portrayal of the clergy, while John Gray's *Men are from Mars, Women are from Venus* has been a bestseller. But the press is another matter. After Khatami's victory in 1997, an explosion of critical newspapers and weeklies burst on to the streets, allowing for unprecedented discussions about social and political issues. And these weren't limited to debates on issues such as feminism, democracy and liberalism, but included new interpretations of Islamic history and culture, and even saw direct and sensitive questions concerning the foreign bank accounts of senior clerics or the behaviour of the intelligence services being asked.

The press captures the mood of widespread dissatisfaction. During a meeting at Tehran University in early August that was organised to celebrate the release from jail of Mohsen Kadivar, a cleric sentenced to 18 months for 'disturbing public opinion', Professor Hashem Aghajaeri was direct: 'Religion has performed badly when it has gone along with

Alborz mountain, Iran: outside Tehran, young men listen to music banned by the Islamic regime.
Credit: Abbas / Magnum

power . . . Those who believe Islamic jurisprudence is a kind of divinity
on earth, that it cannot be criticised, or judged by the law, must enter
debates with Islamic thinkers and let voters choose. Governments that
suppress free thinking under the name of religion are not only not
religious governments but are not even humane governments. It is time
for the institution of religion to become separated from the institution
of government.' His audience of 1,000 students were reported to have
applauded vigorously (*International Herald Tribune*, 5–6 August 2000).

But those opposed to change have fought back: independent writers
have been charged by clerical courts with opposing Islam and the
revolution, and in 1998, a spate of assassinations of writers was blamed

Akbar Ganji in court.
Credit: European
Press Agency

on rogue elements within the security forces. In 1999 there were clashes between students and the security forces and, since 2000, the clampdown has become even heavier. After attending a conference on Iran, held last April in the Heinrich Böll Institute, Berlin, several participants were arrested and tried on returning to Tehran. Among those detained were two supporters of women's rights, Mehrangiz Kar and Shahla Lahiji; a leader of the student organisation Daftar-i Tahkim-i Vahdat (The Office for the Strengthening of Unity); Hojjatislam Hasan Eshkevari, a reformist cleric; and the editors of three newspapers, Reza Jalaipour of *Asr-i Azadegan* (Age of the Free), Ezzatollah Sahabi of *Iran-i Farda* (Tomorrow's Iran), and Alireza Alavitabar of *Subh-i Emruz* (This Morning), all of which were subsequently banned. But the most prominent of those arrested was Akbar Ganji, a journalist who had exposed the involvement of high-ranking officials in the killing of intellectuals. He was sentenced to ten years' imprisonment, followed by five years of exile in a remote village.

As in other authoritarian systems, external threat has been used to justify internal repression: but here too some relaxation is evident. The changes in regard to external relations are in some respects more consolidated. As the country marked in September 2000 the twentieth anniversary of the outbreak of the war with Iraq, Tehran was dominated by giant posters celebrating the 'holy defence' of the country against attack. There were, by comparison, few images of the revolution itself. Posters and paintings commemorated the soldiers who died in the eight-year war, as well as a group of Iranian diplomats killed by the Taliban in 1998. This commemoration of the war was, however, not only a way of remembering the past and mobilising support for the state; it also served to mark out a possible future line for Iranian foreign policy. There is a tangible sense of nationalism and the need to identify what is in Iran's 'national interest' in the atmosphere. And the turn to nationalism has wider implications, both for Iran's support for broader 'Islamic' causes and for the tenor of internal debate.

Iran's Islamic Revolution replicates in its rhetoric and action many of the tensions that beset other revolutions: internationalist militancy and defence of the state, appeals to other oppressed peoples and exaltation of their own people. The French Revolution proclaimed *la grande nation*. Two centuries later, posters in Tehran recall the words of Ayatollah Khomeini, who referred to Iran as *in mellat-i bozorg* 'this great nation'. The Iranian Revolution also replicated in its cultural policy some of what China had gone through. Iranian intellectuals sardonically remark, with regard to the current climate of oppression, that their country did the reverse of China: it has its '100 Flowers Campaign' after its 'cultural revolution'. In China, the campaign of 1957, a persecution of those previously allowed to speak freely, was followed by an all-out onslaught in the Cultural Revolution that began in 1965. The Iranian cultural revolution, launched as an attack on the universities in 1980, served, however, not only to attack 'foreign' ideas and influences, its stated purpose, but also to destroy a diversity of tradition and culture within the country itself. In Iran, this entailed an assault on the more hedonistic trends in Persian poetry, a ban on women singing and even, for a short time, a ban on chess.

As befell earlier revolutionary regimes, the Iranian state is now aware that in the early years of power it paid a high price, not only for its repression at home, but also for exporting revolution to other states. In private, officials recognise two mistakes in particular: the seizure and occupation of the US embassy in November 1979, and the failure to make peace with Iraq in July 1982. The US embassy compound in the city centre is still used by the revolutionary guards, its walls covered with anti-imperialist posters. Yet henceforward, it is implied, interest rather than ideology will prevail. One result of this new approach is a desire to improve relations with the Arab world: Khomeini refused to use the term 'Saudi Arabia', referring to it as 'the so-called Kingdom of Najd and Hijaz', but there has been a significant improvement in relations with Riyadh, and diplomatic ties with Egypt and Algeria, hitherto denounced as secularist oppressors, have been renewed.

One Arab country that Iran has not improved relations with is Iraq: the twin objects of US dual containment always judged it wiser to try to portray the other as the real enemy of international stability rather than to band together, and both still support opposition groups committed to the overthrow of the other's regime. Although Iranian pilgrims and traders now visit Baghdad and Shi'ite shrines in Iraq, the rhetorical war continues: Saddam has, in recent months, stepped up anti-Iranian

*Tehran 2000: erotic pictures from the Rubaiyat return to street stalls in the capital.
Credit: Abbas / Magnum*

propaganda. Iran knows that, in the longer run, a revived Iraq may turn
on it again, as it did in 1980.

The rethinking of foreign policy is, therefore, part of the broader debate
within Iran about the future of the Islamic Republic itself. Here there is
much talk of democratisation and of *jame-yi madani* (civil society). On three
occasions in the past century Iranian society has erupted in protest from
below: in the Constitutional Revolution of 1906, when up to 15,000
protesters took refuge in the spacious 40-acre grounds of the British
embassy; in the period of nationalist prime minister Mosadeq (1951–53);
and in the months preceding and following the fall of the Shah (1978–79).
Each of these earlier experiments in civil society was crushed – the first
two with active foreign intervention. The question now is whether this
will happen again. The Iranian debate involves much speculation on the
preconditions for democracy itself and familiar obstacles are encountered:
if decades ago these were 'imperialism', or 'oriental despotism', the current
favourite is that Iran, by dint of its oil, is a 'rentier' society. For the more
secular, the problem is the undemocratic nature of the clergy itself.

Equally important for today's debate is the legacy that history has left
in the field of literature and social criticism. Throughout modern times,
Iran has had a vibrant literary culture; one that draws on the writings
of the Persian past, but interacts with western literature. In the 1950s
and 1960s there was a vigorous translation of western writings, limited

only by censorship of those works, such as *Macbeth* or *Hamlet*, which portrayed the slaying of a monarch. Much, but not all, of this writing was influenced by Marxism of an orthodox communist kind: Gorky, Sartre and Jack London were favourite authors. Many of these writers were critical of both forms of conservatism afflicting the country, that of the Shah's regime and that of the Islamic clergy. Yet this engagement with modernism from abroad was accompanied by an effervescence within the clerical world that found its expression in the revolution of 1979.

Opponents of change accuse the reformist writers of being 'against Islam'. Ayatollah Khamenei declared, in his letter to the *majlis* last August: 'If the enemies infiltrate the press, this will be a big danger to the country's security and the people's religious beliefs.' Others speak of the 'silent aggression' and 'cultural aggression' coming from abroad. Yet what is not at stake is the Islamic character of the state itself, in the sense that broad respect for Islamic values still exists. In the south of the city a huge complex is being built around the tomb of Khomeini, who died in 1989, and people there talk of turning it into one of the great pilgrimage sites of Islam, along with Mecca, Jerusalem and the Shi'ite shrines. Over it hangs the red flag of Imam Hussein, grandson of the Prophet Muhammad and the founder of Shi'ite Islam who died in 680. Crowds, many from Central Asia, throng the approaches. One man I spoke to, a 28-year-old chauffeur, expressed his criticism of the current elite through his praise for Khomeini: 'The *Imam* was a straightforward man, he did not lie. He was not like the others,' he said.

Twenty years of economic mismanagement and political repression, and a growing contempt for the corruption associated with many of the clergy, have led a shift of opinion within the country. How far this will go no one can tell. Some restrictions – on women's dress codes, for example – have been eased, but the country is still far from allowing the kind of mixture of Islamic and western clothing that is common in other Muslim states, such as Egypt. The protest movement is influenced by economic aspirations and by a western world seen through videos and magazines, and familiar from the large post-revolutionary diaspora.

It is unclear, however, what people want and how far even Khatami is prepared to go. Certainly more than two decades after the revolution, the old slogans no longer work. The economy is not delivering, and there is widespread unemployment. Many of those who supported the revolution and fought Iraq are now disillusioned. Younger people are resisting the social restrictions imposed by the state. There is a huge hunger for political freedom and free speech. Reports suggest that, far from this being confined to Tehran, the feeling of protest is even stronger outside the capital. In early August riots broke out in the southern city of Khorramshahr, scene of some of the heaviest fighting in the Iran–Iraq war, when members of the *pasdaran* (revolutionary guard) attacked a reformist meeting.

This is not, therefore, a conventional situation of social protest challenging a state – the division runs within each. The movement from below faces a state that is divided within itself. Against the reformist movement is ranged a coalition of clerical power associated with *faqih* (spiritual leader) Ayatollah Khamenei, plus some elements in the army, backed by conservative militia forces. The position of the *faqih* has become the most controversial in Iran: reformers want the position curtailed and subject to election, conservatives shout the slogan 'Death to the those who are against the *faqih*'. The clergy are, as they were in the revolution, divided; some favour social and political reform. Some even blame the revolution for discrediting Islam in the eyes of the population.

One of the most militant critics of the regime, Abdullah Nuri, was imprisoned after a trial in which he openly questioned the clerical hold on power and denounced the corruption and abuse of office of his fellow mullahs. Others are deeply entrenched in the regime and have acquired wealth and power through it: they are now a financial as well as a cultural force, and do not wish to lose their power or privileges. One of the leading clerics is clear enough: according to Ayatollah Jannati, 'You cannot save Islam with liberalism and tolerance.' True to ideological type, Jannati went on to question whether, in an Islamic republic, there was a need for novels.

President Khatami himself has wished so far to maintain a coalition with Khamenei. Many of his followers do not want this to continue. In August 2000, when Khamenei intervened in parliament to stop a liberal press law from being passed, he caused great anger within the reformist camp. If Khatami does not press ahead with his reform, then he runs the risk of losing support and facing increased criticism. If he breaks with Khamenei, then there is a risk of a confrontation with the clerical-security complex that opposed him. The followers of Khatami do not want violence, but those opposed to reform are prepared to use it, as they have shown in the past. It is believed that the reformers have the upper hand in the armed forces and the ministry of intelligence, and that a majority of the revolutionary guards voted for reformist candidates in the *majlis* elections: but the judiciary and some of the security forces remain opposed to change.

At the moment there is a ceasefire in the war between reformers and conservatives. The great popular expectations that accompanied the *majlis* elections of February have faded. Several of the leading figures of the Dovvom-i Khordad reform movement, clergy and other intellectuals, are in prison, even while their books are on sale across Tehran. There is uncertainty about the economy, and about Khatami's ability to push through economic reform: this is all the more difficult because some of those who favour the liberalisation of social and political life are as opposed to liberalisation of the economy as they are to any examination of human rights abuses. One particular issue of contention is foreign investment: Iran is not offering international oil and gas firms the production-sharing agreements that other producer states do, and there is little sign that there is sufficient political support for this at the moment.

Barring unexpected developments, the next great test of the reform movement will come in June this year, with the new round of presidential elections. Khatami has stated that he may stand for a second term, and most people expect him to do so. If he runs, it is unlikely that any serious candidate could compete against him. But supporters of former president Rafsanjani may put forward a candidate, possibly former foreign minister Velayati. More important, however, Khatami may not be able to keep the support of those who have, up to now, supported him. The next few months will be decisive for the future direction of Iran and for the fate of the revolutionary regime. Only when they are over will we know the fate of Iran's fourth great experiment in civil society. Whatever happens, Iran's writers and journalists will have plenty to say about these developments: what is not clear is whether these words will find their way into print. ❏

Fred Halliday is *professor of International Relations at the London School of Economics. His latest book is* Nation and Religion in the Middle East *(Saqi £29.50 h/b; £14.95 p/b)*

NED THOMAS

Speech laws

Europe is changing from a collection of citizens with individual rights to a mosaic of language groups with collective rights

Where language is concerned, the rhetoric of the European Union is pluralist. How could it be anything else? No one is going to propose the assimilation of its various peoples to one single language. At the level of European institutions, all kinds of compromise take place, but at the level of citizenship the idea of equality prevails and must prevail if Europe is to have legitimacy. Citizens cannot be treated as inferior because their first language is Finnish or Danish or Dutch. But what of speakers of languages that were accorded a lesser status – or none at all – in the process of constructing nation states? These were once called 'lesser-used languages' in euro-jargon, but now increasingly 'regional and/or minority languages'.

The relationship between languages and language groups is inevitably a relationship of power, so it is not surprising that the terms we use to describe categories of language have political overtones and implications. 'Minority languages' may at first suggest that we are dealing with numbers; Icelandic, a state language overwhelmingly dominant on its own territory, has fewer than half the number of speakers of Welsh, but it is Welsh that is the minority language. Danish is not a minority language in Denmark though it has fewer speakers than Catalan, which is a minority language in three states – France, Spain and Italy (there is a small Catalan enclave on Sardinia).

In some countries, activists prefer to speak of 'minoritised languages' – *langues minorisées* – thus making the point that the group has been *turned* into a minority by the drawing of boundaries in a particular way, or by the exclusion of a language from education or public administration. They call for 'normalisation' of their languages, equality of status with the state language and the ability to live one's life normally

Finland: Sami-speaking herdsmen in Lapland. Credit: © Jim Holmes / Panos Pictures

through one's own language on one's own territory. A minority language, from this point of view, is one that has less promotion than the state language, but which belongs historically to a given territory within the state.

The term 'endangered languages' has an ecological ring to it and is most used for indigenous languages outside Europe, but sometimes also for the Saterfrisians or the Sami language groups in the far north of Europe. Their tiny size might seem, from afar, to make them the most endangered. But in practice, language is so interwoven with every aspect of political, economic and institutional structures that one cannot decide on the basis of size which is most at risk.

A small language group on a clearly defined territory which it does not share with other languages, with a high level of autonomy and guaranteed linguistic rights – such as the 25,000 Swedish-speakers on the Åland Islands in Finland – need not be considered endangered at all.

A small group in a remote area *without* such guarantees may still survive as a communal language unless it proves fatally vulnerable to the discovery of an oilfield, the introduction of an airbase, the incursion of mass tourism or even the building of a good road. This could well be the factor that wipes out the last Greek-speaking villages in Calabria, the descendants of the Greek colonies of antiquity.

Language groups living in a mixed-language situation may, at a particular time, be more endangered than smaller pockets of dense and cohesive population. The Sorbs, speakers of two variants of a Slavonic language near the Czech and Polish borders of the former East Germany, mostly live in areas of mixed population alongside German speakers, and their situation, despite a reasonable level of official support, is precarious.

But support for the minority language sometimes comes from a much larger group that identifies with a language that it does not speak. Thus, the Basque autonomous area of Spain, where the Basque language was severely repressed in Franco's day, has Spanish as the language of the majority, but this majority has the political will to restore the national language and is having a high degree of success in doing so. The same phenomenon can be observed at a lower level in my own country, Wales.

There are minority language groups whose language is nowhere the language of a state – these include most of those mentioned so far – but there are also minority language groups whose language is a state language in another country. In western Europe one can mention the Danish-speaking group in Germany and the German-speaking groups in Denmark, Belgium and the South Tyrol within Italy. Since the break-up of Yugoslavia, the Slovenes in Austria and Italy have a fully-fledged independent state over the border in Slovenia using their language.

The histories of these two types of linguistic minority are in many respects different. The first type has often been marginalised in the historical process of constructing a centralised nation state, and has never had the support of a state for its culture. The elites of those language groups often played a prominent part in the centralising and imperial endeavour – this was certainly true in the UK, France and Spain – but the price paid was assimilation to whichever language the central power adopted. At some point, this assimilation was seen to threaten the very existence of the language group and a reaction set in, with movements dedicated to re-establishing their languages in all the fields from which they had been excluded.

In central and eastern Europe and the CIS countries of the former Soviet Union, the concept of 'national minority' rather takes over from the purely 'linguistic minority'. An ethnic and religious, as well as a linguistic dimension may enter the legal definition and self-perception of the group; indeed the 'ethnic' definition may outlive the linguistic one. By no means all the Volga Germans allowed to migrate to Germany could still speak German, and very few Ingermanlanders (a group speaking a language akin to Finnish in an area close to the former Leningrad until dispersed by Stalin) could speak anything but Russian when accepted by Finland. This emphasis on ethnic group is more alien to western European minorities of the first type, who take pleasure in demonstrating that Chinese, Thai or, indeed, US children have all gone successfully through the Welsh or Catalan school system and become part of the language community.

There is one category for which I find no accepted name – it includes Scots and Platt-Deutsch, and possibly Occitan in the southern half of France. On a narrow and purist definition, few people speak these languages all the time – group consciousness is not very strong and neither is the modern spoken standard. But on a broad definition these are very large groups – sleeping giants who might in certain circumstances mobilise around language. Ulster Scots – a very small group indeed, which few people had heard of ten years ago – ended up being included in the Anglo-Irish Agreement as a counterweight to the Irish language. The distinction between dialect and language will never be settled on a purely academic basis, but will fluctuate with the many political and economic processes in which societies and languages are caught up.

Does it make sense to group these very various kinds of minority together at all? Despite very different situations, there are almost always, at the level of individuals and groups, experiences of linguistic discrimination, often producing internalised feelings of inferiority with which virtually every linguistic minority will identify. It is calculated that some 40–50 million EU citizens have as their language one that is not the official language of their nation state. The many regions where these languages are spoken have considerable representation in the European Parliament and have had a limited success in keeping the question of linguistic minorities on the agenda.

It is due to pressure by Parliament and the European Bureau for Lesser-Used Languages that Article 22 of the Charter of Fundamental

Region	Potentially endangered *Languages with a substantial number of adult and child speakers, but without official status.*	Endangered *Languages with a large number of adult speakers, but a decreasing number of child speakers.*
Arctic		North Sámi
Balkans		Aromunian, Arbëreshë Albanian
Baltics		Karelian (proper), Olonetsian
Benelux		Western Frisian, Walloon
Black Sea		Rusyn, Gagauz, Kalmyk
British Isles	Lowland Scots	Scottish Gaelic, Welsh
France	Galician, Franco-Provençal, Occitan	Provençal, Gascon
Mediterranean & Italy	Piedmontese, Ligurian, Lombard, Emilian, Corsican	Cimbrian, Algherese Catalan, Ladin, Friulian, Gallurese Sardinian, Logudorese Sardinian, Campidanese Sardinian, Sassarese Sardinian
Poland, Austria & Germany	Low Saxon	Lower Sorbian, Upper Sorbian, Burgenland Croatian, Romansch
Russia	Belorussian	Erzya, Moksha, Eastern Mari, Udmurt, Permyak, Komi (proper), Tundra Nenets, Chuvash, Bashkir, Nogai, Trukhmen
Spain & Portugal		Asturian, Aragonese, Basque, Catalan
Non-territorial		Romani

Seriously endangered	Nearly extinct	Extinct
Languages with a sizeable number of speakers, but who are exclusively elderly.	*Languages with a maximum of ten speakers.*	*Languages that are no longer spoken (excluding ancient dialects).*
South Sámi, Lule Sámi, Inari Sámi, Skolt Sámi, Kildin Sámi	Ume Sámi, Pite Sámi. Akkala Sámi, Ter Sámi	Kemi Sámi, Southern Mansi
Molise Croatian, Istriot, Istro-Romanian, Meglenitic, Arvanitika Albanian, Tsakonian, Pontic Greek	Yevanic (Judeo-Greek)	Dalmatian
Ingrian, Ludian	Livonian, Votian	
Karaim, Crimean Tatar	Krimchak (Judeo-Crimean Tatar)	Gothic, Southern Mansi
		Manx Gaelic, Cornish, Norn
Breton, Languedocien, Auvergnat, Limousin, Channel Island French		Shuadit (Judeo-Provençal), Zarphatic (Judeo-French)
Italiot Greek, Cypriot Arabic	Italkian (Judeo-Italian)	
Yiddish (Judeo-German), Kashubian (proper), Eastern Frisian, Northern Frisian		Old Prussian, Polabian, Slovincian
Vepsian, Western Mari		
Leonese, Ladino (Judeo-Spanish) Classical Greek		Mozarabic

Information predominantly supplied by Tapani Salminen, UNESCO. Compiled by DG

Rights, adopted at the Nice Summit in December 2000, states that 'The Union shall respect cultural, religious and linguistic diversity'. Article 21 prohibits discrimination, mentioning, among other grounds, language and membership of national minorities. These are very weak references in a Charter that itself has no binding effect – but it represents a small triumph for a view of Europe not as a collection of citizens with individual human rights, but as a mosaic of linguistic groups with collective rights.

The Council of Europe's Charter of Regional and/or Minority Languages is a stronger document, focused wholly on language. It requires undertakings to promote and support the languages in question in areas such as education, media and public life. It also has its weaknesses, of course. States are allowed to sign up at different levels so have usually chosen the level of their existing provision. The Charter only moves things forward in those places where minority language groups had few or no guaranteed rights. Politically it was driven forward with central and eastern Europe in mind, and by the desire to avoid further conflicts such as that in Kosovo which, in its earlier stages, was fuelled by linguistic discrimination.

But once signed and ratified by a country, the Charter is legally binding and should guarantee a minimum of respect for linguistic rights. A majority of EU countries (and many outside the EU) have signed it, though some are dragging their feet on ratification. In France, the Constitutional Council declared Prime Minister Lionel Jospin's signature of the Charter unconstitutional, and it is likely to be some years before Greece – the most hostile of EU countries towards its minorities – can be persuaded to conform to a EU norm. But even in Greece public opinion is changing.

In recent years, the UK has had a relatively good record in its treatment of its autochthonous, linguistic minorities, but always on an ad hoc and concessionary rather than juridical basis. Continental Europe sees itself, naturally, as a mosaic of linguistic groups, each with its own territory, though there may be arguments about where the borders of those territories lie. The Anglo-Saxon tradition, by contrast, has great difficulty in granting collective rights to a given group on a given territory. Linguistic questions here are constantly confused with race relations, and individual rights with group rights. What is needed is a direct dialogue between immigrant minorities and autochthonous minorities. Their histories, aspirations and linguistic demands are quite different, but confusing one category with the other – the mosaic with the melting pot – helps no one.

In Europe the redrawing of state boundaries has been abandoned as a means of settling minority questions. There are too many historical skeletons to commend that approach. The problems that arise are instead addressed through the encouragement of regional autonomy – which has come about for a variety of other reasons as well – and through the guaranteeing of rights by international charters and conventions.

The creation of regional autonomies solves some problems but can generate others. It has generally been a positive development in Spain, but some minorities are too small to be anything but minorities within very small regions – the Slovenes in Jörg Haider's Carinthia, for example. In other places the regional and administrative structure is organised so as to divide speakers of the same minority language between different administrative areas. In France, for example, the government has resisted redrawing administrative boundaries to create a Basque *département*; in Italy, Slovenes and Ladino-speakers are divided between different jurisdictions with different levels of rights. Then again, what of the minorities *within* a minority language area? Catalunya has accorded very full linguistic rights to Occitan in Val d'Aran.

The Charters are overarching European guarantees. They are of course only as good as the monitoring systems established to check on performance – and the political resolve of Europe to deal with offenders. But something is being slowly set in place that may help to right old wrongs and give Europe a better name in the rest of the world. ❏

Ned Thomas is academic director of the Mercator Centre at the University of Wales, Aberystwyth, which runs projects concerned with linguistic minorities, media, literature and translation

Identikit Europe

**A state of mind?
A place?
A people?
Who is Europe?**

Paris, France: life on the Euro-go-round.
Credit: © Richard Kalvar / Magnum

NORMAN STONE

Eurokid and Colonel Blimp

National identity goes far deeper than a European one and, if we want to avoid a nationalist backlash as in Austria, it would be better for us to live with that reality

When Germany surrendered on 8 May 1945, Berlin was, famously, an enormous ruin – a moonscape. Within two days, the first underground trains ran again. At the same moment, the buses in victorious London were on strike. It was a parable of the entire post-war era. The low point was reached in the later 1970s when, by most measurements, the British were about half as prosperous as the Germans; even well-intentioned German students spending time in Edinburgh were rather shocked at the level of poverty they experienced.

Wandering around Stirling as the dusk gathered, and shutting your ears to the language, you might have thought you were in some Iron Curtain wasteland – a Kielce in Poland, a Zaporzhiye in Ukraine. The West Germans had also experienced a problem of heavy industrial run-down, in their case in the Ruhr, which had once been the coal and steel powerhouse of the continent. By agreement of all parties concerned – government, unions, bosses – they had seen the problem and headed off its nastiest manifestations. Essen, with new educational institutions, museums, parks and an impressive set of new roads, was a decent place to live, in huge contrast, say, to Sheffield in contemporary England, let alone Liverpool. You went into a pub, and saw there much the same proletarian faces as you did in northern England at the time: tipsy, frizzy-haired women whose faces showed that they had been through the mill. The difference from England was that the faces had hope. Life was not just ghastly concrete estates, 'benefits' and vandalism.

London 1940s: café society in the ghost of a bar. Credit: © Philip Jones Griffiths / Magnum

What made for the Germans' post-war recovery? One thing does stand out: Europe. In 1950, the French proposed a Coal and Steel Community, which had the initial advantage that the Ruhr powerhouse would be under international, rather than German, control. A subsidiary advantage was that French steel-makers, who were backward and fearful of competition, could be persuaded, by the nationalist argument, to submit to competition. It did them a world of good – it was in fact a chief factor in the French recovery that followed so spectacularly. For the Germans, the advantage lay in respectability; they could work their passage, through 'Europe', and it also meant a much larger market. To

STRIPSEARCH by Martin Rowson

"OF COURSE IT IS ABSOLUTELY LUDICROUS TO IMPUTE ANY RACIST AGENDA TO OUR CEASELESS EFFORTS TO PREVENT OUR ALREADY OVER-CROWDED WESTERN EUROPEAN HOMELAND FROM BEING SWAMPED BY BOGUS ASYLUM SEEKERS AND ECONOMIC MIGRANTS, BE THEY FROM THE FORMER YUGOSLAVIA..."

"...OR JEWS..."

"...OR TURKS..."

this day – or at any rate until two or three years ago – Germans were clamantly 'European': 'a European Germany, not a German Europe', as Chancellor Kohl, quoting Thomas Mann, used to say. Take a critical stance towards the European Union in modern German politics and you get nowhere. It was in vain that the 40 senior economists in the Federal Republic protested against the introduction of a European currency without proper safeguards, just as in 1990 they had protested against the one-for-one exchange of the almost valueless East German mark for the hard-currency West German one. They were waved aside by politicians; and though the German public are largely unenthusiastic, they do not assert their lack of enthusiasm in actual voting power.

Contrast this with England (Scotland is rather different). With large majorities, public opinion goes against European union – it is almost unanimously hostile to a European federal state, three-quarters hostile to a European currency, while widespread resentment against such measures as the conversion of weights and measures into continental equivalents also exists. Foreign languages are a disaster area, far more so than in 1914, when three members of the cabinet that went to war with Germany had studied at the then famous German universities. The tabloids never really miss a chance to mock the French or the Germans;

sometimes, it seems that the only two European peoples for whom the English have any time are the Dutch and the Russians.

Much of this, we might as well concede, is hopelessly irrational. Exposure to continental European competition did the British economy a world of good: if, say, British Steel became a success story, it was because the old problems of overmanning, mistaken investment and lavish subsidy had to be overcome if the industry were not to collapse altogether. The same has been true of inward investment – again, an important cause of the British recovery in the 1980s. We would probably never have changed our ways had it not been for the competition from Europe, or the attractiveness of that vast market. And yet ignorance, or hostility, are the most common English reactions. Why? And is it, in the end, healthy?

Jean Monnet was right when he said that the British would never really see the point of 'Europe' because they had not been invaded, and experienced that humiliation at first hand. But, beyond that, English and continental history took a sharply different turn: institutions that on the continent were fossils were, in England, well and truly alive. Much of what we regard as ineradicably English is in fact pre-Absolutist European. 'The Common Law', for instance, is a version of *ius commune*

(Roman Law), updated as and when necessary, and common to western Europe until Absolutist and Enlightenment rulers started to upset it in the name of rationalism. Ideas such as 'freehold' are only barely translatable into continental languages, and people do not know what they signify. Even serfdom was not formally abolished in England until the 1930s, though by then, and for centuries past, it had only involved a particular type of property, by which, say, a retired farm labourer had a cottage in return for mowing a lawn or looking after the dogs. There was no *académie britannique* to standardise spelling; Oxford and Cambridge, with colleges that are essentially medieval, were never centralised and modernised at bayonet point, as happened with Louvain or the Sorbonne.

'Why?' is a good question for English historians, and those with a good (or sometimes direct) knowledge of Europe – Frederick Maitland, Lewis Namier and Geoffrey Elton are the most obvious names – each had his answer. Elton, pointing to the Tudor dissolution of the monasteries, is convincing. On the Continent, the church held about one-third of the land, and looked after education and charity. Come the dissolution of the monasteries, England was compelled to find different answers: the Elizabethan Poor Law, 'public' schools, colleges in Oxford and Cambridge that were often built out of the proceeds of confiscated monasteries. Absolutism, even the formal Enlightenment of the eighteenth century, did not occur in England because they were unnecessary. What do you make of a country, I often ask my Turkish students, which by 50 years was the first to abolish slavery, and by 80 the last to abolish serfdom?

Insistence on the uniqueness of England is therefore not wrong, and whatever the benefits the country had from joining the European Union in 1972, the popular reaction is more soundly based than is, say, the Europhile presentation of my old friend Norman Davies in his recent book *The Islanders*. He makes the point that, in the Middle Ages, the language of the court was Norman French; he makes the further point that England absorbed the Celtic fringe, Scotland and Wales, whereas these countries, left to themselves, could easily have found some European identity. It is a discussion point, and Scotland, poorer than England, was indeed compelled to use the machinery of the state for enlightened purposes because there was not, as in England, a rich aristocracy or a City to produce the schools and the canals and the roads and the agricultural improvements on their own. *Am Anfang war Napoleon* – 'in the beginning was Napoleon' – is the start of a famous multi-volume history of modern Germany by Thomas Nipperday. You could, maybe, use it also to start a multi-volume history of modern Europe, and it would even, quite neatly, define today's Europe, in the sense that it follows quite closely the boundaries of the countries that accepted Napoleon's Continental System in 1808. But it would not fit the British Isles at all, except maybe for a few Irish rebels and the shadowy Jacobite claimant, a cardinal living in Rome.

It is, no doubt, ungrateful of the British not to recognise what Europe has done for them, and it is carping of them to point to this or that defect in the European machine (all that money stolen). It is, no doubt, ungenerous of them to say that the European army would just be 'camping with attitude'. But there it is: I doubt if the British are going to be changed very much by preaching. And, in the end, it is healthier that they should remain, as a mass, fairly sceptical about the whole venture.

The real danger with Europe is surely that it will be unable to stop itself from trying to do too much. That is, in a way, the great danger with hurriedly built unities of this sort. When Italy was created, in 1860–61, there were, by universal confession, few true Italians. Francesco Crispi, an imperialist-minded prime minister in the 1890s, said that he would make Italy run (with an empire) so that she would at least learn to walk (with a state). Of post-Bismarckian Germany you might say the same; and in both cases the results were a disaster for the twentieth century. Nowadays, we have a Europe that is indeed, whatever spokesmen say, an attempted state-identity: an army, a foreign policy, a parliament, an anthem, a passport, a currency and even a unified tax scheme. The danger of a nationalist backlash is palpable – hence the absurd overreaction to the Austrians' promotion of Jörg Haider in an obviously impeccable democratic process. The problem is that national identity goes far, far deeper than a European one, and it would be better for us to live with that reality. As John Maynard Keynes (1883–1946) wrote, seeing the disarray of the left-wing intelligentsia in the *New Statesman*, 'three cheers for Colonel Blimp'. We might yet need him. ❏

Norman Stone *is Professor of International Relations at Bilkent University, Ankara. He taught for many years at Oxford and Cambridge and is about to produce a new book,* The Atlantic Revival 1970–1990

VACLAV HAVEL

Fact or fiction?

The best as well as the worst of twentieth-century experiences have been generated in Europe

Do Europe's peoples truly regard themselves as 'Europeans', or is this simply a fiction that attempts to transform geography into a 'state of mind'?

When I ask myself to what extent I feel European, and what links me with Europe, I am mildly astonished at the fact that it is only now that I ponder the question. Why didn't I think of it long ago? Was it because I regarded my belonging to Europe as a surface matter of little significance? Or did I take my European identity for granted?

My entire background was so self-evidently European that it never occurred to me to probe my thoughts. Not only that: I have a feeling that I would have looked ridiculous if I had written or declared that I was European and felt European, or professed explicitly a European orientation. Such manifestations would have appeared pathetic and pompous; a loftier version of the kind of patriotism that I dislike in national patriots.

Such hesitation apparently holds true for most Europeans: they are so intrinsically European that they are unaware of it. Conscious Europeanism has little tradition, so I welcome the fact that European awareness is rising from the indistinct mass of the self-evident. This is immensely important – especially since we find ourselves in a multicultural, multipolar world in which recognising one's own identity is a prerequisite for co-existence with others.

If Europe, until recently, paid so little attention to its own identity, it was because it saw itself as the entire world, considered itself to be so superior to the rest of the globe that it felt no need to define itself in relation to others. Inevitably, this had unfortunate consequences on its behaviour.

Reflecting on Europeanism means enquiring into the set of values, ideals and principles that characterise Europe. It entails, by definition, a critical examination of that set of thoughts, followed by the realisation that many European traditions, principles or values may be double-edged. Some, if carried too far or abused in certain ways, can lead us to hell.

In this effort of reflection, emphasis must be placed on the spiritual dimension and the underlying values of European integration. Until now, European unification, and its meaning in the wider context of civilisation, has been hidden behind technical, economic, financial and administrative issues.

Jewish school, Paris: the values of infancy.
Credit: © Martine Franck / Magnum

When unification began after World War II, democratic western Europe was faced with the memory of the horrors of two world wars and the threat of communist totalitarian rule. Back then, there was no need to speak of the values to be defended, because these were self-evident. The West had to unite to prevent the spread of dictatorship, as well as the danger of a relapse into old national conflicts.

In its infancy, the European Union had much the same attitude to its European identity as I to my own. Europe's moral justification was self-evident; it did not need to be professed. Because western Europe was defending something equally self-evident, there was no need to describe or analyse it. It was not until the physical threat to Europe disappeared just over a decade ago that Europe was prompted to engage in profound reflections upon the moral and spiritual foundations of its unification, and what the objectives of a united Europe should be.

The basic set of European values formed by the spiritual and political history of the continent is clear. It consists of respect for the individual and for humanity's freedoms, rights and dignity; the principle of solidarity; the rule of law and equality before the law; protection of minorities; democratic institutions; separation of legislative, executive

Britain 1992: UK citizens from Asia enjoy a day on the beach in Wales.
Credit: © David Hurn / Magnum

and judicial powers; political pluralism; respect for private ownership and private enterprise, and a market economy; and the furtherance of civil society. These values mirror countless modern European experiences, including the fact that our continent is now a multicultural crossroads.

In defining what it means to be 'European', a crucial task is to reflect upon the double-edged nature of what we have given the world, to realise that Europe not only taught the world about human rights, but also introduced the Holocaust; that we generated spiritual impulses not only for the industrial and information revolutions, but also to plunder and contaminate nature; that we incited the advance of science and technology, but also ruthlessly ousted essential human experiences forged over several millennia.

The worst events of the twentieth century – world wars, fascism, communist totalitarianism – were mostly Europe's doing. During the last century, however, Europe also experienced three auspicious events, though all were not exclusively European accomplishments: the end of colonial rule; the fall of the Iron Curtain; the beginning of European integration.

A fourth great task lies ahead. Through the manner of its being, a unifying Europe must demonstrate that the dangerous contradictions inherent in its civilisation can be combated. ❏

Vaclav Havel is president of the Czech Republic. Reproduced courtesy © Project Syndicate

MARTIN WOOLLACOTT

Soft cop, hard cop

The launch of the new Euro-army raises critical questions about its value on a continent which, since Kosovo, lacks any comparable doorstep cases

A once popular French print entitled *Sous les Ailes*, produced just before World War I, shows rank after rank of blue-coated troops advancing across cornfields. Above them soars one of the new aeroplanes; above that, in a ghostly tableau amid the clouds, Napoleon's cavalry form for battle; above them in turn the imperial eagle spreads its wings. Such evocations of glory, history and the mission of arms were once commonplace across Europe. Not so now, but the identity, morale and even the appearance of European soldiers – all the little curiosities of their uniforms, badges and flags – are nevertheless rooted in the victories and defeats not only of the two great wars, but of a more distant past.

Yet one of the paradoxes of modern European history is that, while there is nothing more national than armed forces, the military experience of Europeans has been much more of alliance than of independent national action and, in the last half-century, predominantly within NATO and the Warsaw Pact. The armed forces of Europe are thus both an obstacle to unity, in that they represent a depository of intensely national feeling, and a way of achieving it, since they are already among the most integrated of European institutions. Military power, directed outwards at the non-European world, and inwards in continental wars, has been a defining characteristic of Europe for centuries.

In recent times, the level of effort and spending during the Cold War was such that most Europeans took it for granted – until the Balkan troubles began – that, for good or ill, military capacity was available if it was thought to be needed. The Americans, of course, had the largest and most sophisticated forces, but the Europeans were not spending that much less and they had, in total, more men and women in uniform than did the US. If left alone by Washington, as they were in the Balkans, they could surely meet the challenge. The military dilemma that now faces Europe emerged when governments and peoples realised the large element of sham in their defence establishments. A mountain of expenditure over the decades had produced a mouse in terms of forces that could actually be deployed.

Some European countries, such as Germany and Italy, had inert conscript armies, just beginning to be reformed, designed only for territorial defence. Britain and France alone had some real capacity to project power, but it was limited in quantity, quality and sustainability. There were yawning gaps in the European inventory that only the US could supply, as the Kosovo operation showed. The failure to cope effectively with Yugoslavia's disintegration had many causes; one was the not easily admitted but increasingly obvious fact that Europe alone did not have the resources to confront Serbia militarily and be sure of a swift and successful outcome. Even those who opposed the recourse to force in the Balkans might accept that it would have been better if it had been more clearly available to Europe as an option.

One leader who saw this was Tony Blair. As the situation in Kosovo worsened in 1998, he abandoned Britain's long-standing opposition to the concept of a European defence identity. Although it was too late to create the capacity that Europe should have had on hand to deal with the Balkan wars, it was not too late to lay the foundations for a capacity that might be ready for the next crisis. Blair was, no doubt, also influenced by the need to play a high card at a time when Britain had ruled out early entry into the common currency.

The resulting rapprochement with the French is not without ambiguities. The British, with the Germans in discreet support, see the project as one which will sustain US engagement in Europe and help NATO survive. Although the French also believe NATO is an indispensable element in European security, their instinct is to push for greater European autonomy and clearer separation of NATO and EU structures. These differences continue a debate that goes back 50 years, but it is now both modified and muted. There has also been a readiness to put aside grand argument and talk instead about getting the men and equipment that are needed, hence the agreements since on the size and composition of the force of 60,000 that is supposed to be ready by 2003.

Sarajevo, Bosnia: French troops train for rapid response.
Credit: Luc Delahaye / Magnum

The partially resolved differences between France and Britain are not the only ones that affect this project. These two countries share a tradition of overseas military intervention now only faintly evident in the Spanish, Dutch, Belgian, Portuguese and Italian cases, and missing entirely in Germany and Scandinavia; the experience of the East Europeans and of the neutral states is to have suffered intervention, rather than take part in it. One Swedish MP recalls that, when he was campaigning for EU membership, the apprehensive question 'Does this mean we will have to join the German army?' was not uncommon.

The range of tasks in which a European force might be involved runs from another operation like Kosovo, where it would operate with the US but play a larger part, to smaller-scale peacekeeping and peace-enforcement missions. But when the attempt is made to identify them more accurately, the problems are clear. Would Germans or Swedes want to take part in an African intervention? Could Germans take part in a Middle Eastern one? More broadly, could unanimity, or anything like it, be achieved in favour of any intervention that seems possible, absent another Kosovo (and it is very hard to see where another Kosovo might occur within Europe and its immediate confines)? And, more broadly still, should military intervention, except in the direst doorstep case, be a European game? There are plenty of advocates of the idea that Europe should be a soft rather than a hard power, dealing in aid and advice rather than offering military solutions.

The attempt to create even this relatively modest force, in other words, suffers from the argument that much effort and money will be expended to create a capacity it would have been very useful to have had in 1991 or 1998, but which is not relevant now. As Germany shows, military reform is slow and painful. It is also expensive. Even though Europe's problem is more one of misallocation of defence funds than of the absolute amount of money available, there will be large extra costs for a difficult five- or ten-year period if even some of the gaps in Europe's defective inventory of weapons and equipment are to be filled.

There are no clear signs that European governments are going to make enough money available, given the other calls on their resources. Nor is there much support from citizens who are capable of being outraged when their countries find themselves without military means, but are unenthusiastic when it is time to pay for them. Europe's military identity is, thus, still a very uncertain thing. The most likely outcome is a typically European one. Some of the money will be found, some of the organisational changes will be brought in, and some of the targets will be genuinely met, but the force will not be fully ready on time, and serious differences will remain as to how and when it might be used.

The completion of France's transition from conscript to professional forces will add to the pool of competent manpower, but a similar German bonus is much further off. Much will depend on the shifting relationship of the US and Europe, and on how crises which cannot now be foreseen shape events. What can be said is that another diplomatic and military failure of the kind that Europe experienced in the Balkans would be catastrophic for the EU, and even a lesser disaster would be very damaging. Ulrich Beck, a German sociologist, greeted the Kosovo intervention as 'the military equivalent of the euro'. It was not yet that, but may come to be seen in the future as a step towards that goal. ❑

Martin Woollacott *is a foreign affairs commentator for the* Guardian

Simon Davies on

PRIVACY

Ursula Owen on

HATE SPEECH

Patricia Williams on

RACE

Gabriel Garcia Marquez on

JOURNALISM

John Naughton on

THE INTERNET

... all in INDEX

SUBSCRIBE & SAVE

UK and overseas

○ **Yes! I want to subscribe to *Index*.**

❒ 1 year (6 issues)	£39	Save 28%
❒ 2 years (12 issues)	£74	Save 31%
❒ 3 years (18 issues)	£102	**You save 37%**

Name

Address

B0B5

£ _____ enclosed.   ❒ Cheque (£)   ❒ Visa/MC   ❒ Am Ex   ❒ Bill me
(Outside of the UK, add £6 a year for foreign postage)

Card No.

Expiry   Signature

❒ I do not wish to receive mail from other companies.

✉ Freepost: INDEX, 33 Islington High Street, London N1 9BR
☎ (44) 171 278 2313   Fax: (44) 171 278 1878
e tony@indexoncensorship.org

SUBSCRIBE & SAVE

North America

○ **Yes! I want to subscribe to *Index*.**

❒ 1 year (6 issues)	$52	Save 21%
❒ 2 years (12 issues)	$96	Save 27%
❒ 3 years (18 issues)	$135	**You save 32%**

Name

Address

B0B5

$ _____ enclosed.   ❒ Cheque ($)   ❒ Visa/MC   ❒ Am Ex   ❒ Bill me

Card No.

Expiry   Signature

❒ I do not wish to receive mail from other companies.

✉ Freepost: INDEX, 708 Third Avenue, 8th Floor, New York, NY 10017
☎ (44) 171 278 2313   Fax: (44) 171 278 1878
e tony@indexoncensorship.org

MARK THOMPSON

Forging peace

Balkan media, particularly the Serbian press, were actively engaged in forging war in the region. Now they have to learn a new role

On 29 September 1997, so the story goes, General Wesley Clark, NATO Supreme Allied Commander, Europe (SACEUR), was scanning transcripts of that morning's press conference in Sarajevo when a detail leaped out at him.

Among the statements by the international organisations that were implementing the Dayton peace agreement in Bosnia and Herzegovina was some strong criticism of SRT, the Bosnian Serb television network. The United Nations spokesman was indignant that SRT's latest coverage of the War Crimes Tribunal in The Hague had been given an anti-Dayton slant.

Clark could not let this pass. The Bosnian Serb hardline leaders had agreed a mere month before to cease their inflammatory broadcasts against the international community. The NATO powers were ready to show that 'persistent and blatant contravention' of the peace process would not be tolerated. On 1 October, despite a hurried apology from SRT, troops from NATO countries took control of four key SRT transmitters. To get use of the transmitters back, SRT had to accept a far-reaching programme of restructuring.

With hindsight, this military operation was a turning point. It meant that the powers then trying to mend the Balkan countries and set them on the road to democracy had at last woken up to the importance of democratising the mass media.

Assistance to the Balkan media had been championed in the early 1990s by non-governmental organisations, from George Soros's Open Society Institute to the tenuous outfits staffed by dedicated activists with hand-to-mouth funding. These NGOs were excellent at supporting professional media. What they could not do – lacking either mandate or resources – was tackle the structural problems that held the media back.

The result was an explosion of private media outlets in a context of outdated socialist legislation, abysmal market conditions and total political control of the main television networks and many leading newspapers. Bosnia and Macedonia gained more broadcasters per capita than anywhere else in Europe, possibly the world.

Then, in 1996, the OSCE (Organisation for Security and Co-operation in Europe) tried to make Bosnia's unruly media contribute to an environment for free and fair elections in September. The wholesale failure of this half-hearted effort persuaded Swedish politician Carl Bildt, the senior international civilian in Bosnia, that his mandate to tackle refractory media must be beefed up. This was done, and six months later the world's most powerful military alliance swung into action.

The following year, in 1998, plans to democratise Bosnia's media were unveiled. Several international organisations combined to start the transformation of the so-called 'state broadcasters' into public-service networks, to liberalise media laws and to mould an effective association of journalists as a first step to raising ethical standards.

Meanwhile, next door in Croatia, the OSCE mission joined with US and European diplomats to push the Tudjman regime on media reform. Croatia's own reformists kept a discreet distance from this external pressure, yet, to judge by the nationalists' heavy defeat in January 2000 elections, it did the liberals and democrats no harm, perhaps some good.

When tiny Montenegro distanced itself from Serbia in 1998, it tried to demonstrate its democratic good intentions in the media sphere. The fall of Milosevic last October awakened interest in bringing Serbia's media laws and institutions into line with European norms. The new OSCE mission in Belgrade is recruiting four or five international staff for its media development unit.

The most controversial effort at media restructuring occurred in Kosovo, where the UN and OSCE were soon accused by media watchdogs in the US, as well as by newspapers such as the *New York Times* and the *Wall Street Journal*, of plotting a neo-colonial domination of the media. When the UN issued a draconian edict against hate-speech, then imposed a regulatory regime for print and broadcast media, it was denounced for making itself prosecutor, judge and jury against local journalists: hardly a model of democratic practice.

Kosovo, 2000: all the news that's fit to watch. Credit: © George Georgiou / Panos Pictures

These concerns were partly resolved by creating an appeals board that proved its independence in September 2000 by annulling the UN-OSCE mission's punishment of a Kosovo newspaper. After this, relations between the mission and the local media settled down. The professional quality of media coverage before elections in November exceeded expectations. The real problems afflicting journalism in Kosovo are lawlessness and poverty rather than international diktat.

The standard-setting agency here is the Council of Europe, working against a background of international instruments such as the European Convention on Human Rights. Sometimes deprecated as a talking shop, the CoE is another intergovernmental organisation that has come into its own since the end of the Cold War. Its experts have travelled widely

in Europe's transitional countries, assessing media laws and proposing
amendments. What they lack in muscle is partly made up in quasi-moral
authority, which resonates loudly in countries that are queuing up to
join the European Union.

But only partly. International efforts at media reform in the
Balkans have been undermined by opportunism. The performance of
governments in the region has not been judged consistently by a set
of agreed standards. On the contrary, criticism waxes and wanes in line
with international priorities across the region. NATO only acted against
SRT to boost a rival Bosnian Serb leader against the hardliners. When
Croatia was under pressure for meddling in Bosnia and blocking the
return of Serb refugees, it was also denounced for repression in the
media. With the election of more pliable leaders, the great powers
lost interest in Croatia's media.

The starkest case of opportunism, however, is provided by
Macedonia. This impoverished country of some 2 million people
has been praised, indeed overpraised for taking a more liberal attitude
to the media. In fact, Macedonia's media are in a chaotic and dangerous
condition. Pluralism is merely numerical, political manipulation is
ubiquitous, and standards both professional and ethical are low. Perhaps
worst of all, the media sector is split along linguistic lines that reflect
all too accurately the parallel ghettos where the ethnic majority
(Macedonians) and largest minority (Albanians) live.

The international community, however, seems indifferent to the
potential of media to bridge this gap. Absorbed in learning the painful
skills of post-conflict peace-building, western governments are still
reluctant to address the needs of active conflict prevention. Some
of the slack can be taken up by NGOs such as the US-based Search
for Common Ground, which pioneered multi-ethnic programming
for children in Macedonia; but engagement at government level is still
needed. ❑

Mark Thompson *is Balkans programme director of the International Crisis
Group. His new book,* Forging Peace: International Intervention, Media
and Conflict, *co-edited with Monroe Price, will be published later this year by
Edinburgh University Press*

Exits & entrances

✦ **To sustain current economic growth, EU countries will need 150 million extra workers over the next 25 years. Germany alone will need to import half a million workers a year.**

✦ **In 1999, 356,960 individuals applied for political asylum in EU countries. 24% of these originated in Yugoslavia.**

✦ **Of all the countries of the EU, Germany has the largest number of asylum seekers awaiting a decision on their fate – 949,240 had yet to be processed by the end of 1999.**

✦ **Of the 91,080 asylum seekers arriving in the United Kingdom in 1999, 1,400 were repatriated.**

France, February 2001: Kurdish shipwreck.
Credit: Camera Press / P H Arnassau /
Varmatin / Imapress

✦ In Italy, 54% of all administrators and managers are women, the highest in the world.

✦ In Poland, Belarus and Ukraine, the average wage for a female employee is up to 80% that of her male counterpart. This compares with just 40% in Ireland.

✦ Homosexuality, legalised throughout the EU, remains illegal or 'immoral' in three European countries: Romania, Bosnia and Macedonia.

✦ Ireland is the only European country in which abortion is forbidden.

✦ Eight European countries retain the death penalty, three of which – Belarus, Russia and Yugoslavia – actively use it. Executions were outlawed by the EU in 1998.

✦ Over three-quarters of Europe's population is of Christian denomination; an estimated 3.2% are affirmed atheists.

✦ The country with the lowest crime rate is Iceland – its only prison holds just 65 convicts, most of whom are 'part-time'.

✦ Germany has the highest level of press freedom in Europe; the lowest is in Belarus.

✦ Only five EU countries – Belgium, Holland, Luxembourg, Ireland and the UK – do not have some form of military service. In Greece, conscientious objectors are liable to four years' imprisonment.

✦ Lithuania boasts the highest suicide rate in Europe: 95 in every 100,000 people end up taking their own lives there. Albania, with 5 suicides per 100,000 citizens, has the lowest rate.

✦ With 525,000 soldiers, Turkey possesses the largest army in Europe. Russia has the biggest armed force on the continent, with over 1,159,000 military personnel. ❏

Sources: UN, EU, Amnesty International, World Health Organisation and others. Compiled by **DG**

JUAN LUÍS CEBRIÁN

Few tongues, many voices?

Even greater concentration of media ownership could be Europe's salvation from homogenised cultural globalisation

For the first time in its history, western Europe is ruled by a generation of people who, until the Kosovo crisis, had never gone to war. This is essential to understanding the problems of our identity. For centuries, this continent has been configured on the basis of confrontation between peoples, religions or races. The 'right to be different' has usually been vindicated with more force than the right to be equal, even in times in which the latter was the most visible revolutionary banner.

Today, most western Europeans are peaceful people. Yet many of them are engaged in a number of cultural struggles. The expression of this right to be different is usually shaped around a culture which, too often, has been identified only with a certain language. This helps explain why newspapers have normally constituted one of the most chauvinistic and nationalistic elements of every European society.

The media have thus often become expressions of the self-identification and even self-satisfaction of the societies in which they are born. The institutionalisation of the press and its often reverential attitude to the powers that be have made it the mouthpiece of national interest.

I remember when the French minister of the interior went to General de Gaulle's office to denounce the attitude of the elderly philosopher Jean-Paul Sartre, then involved in public agitation in favour of the most radical causes. He suggested arresting him, however painful and scandalous that might be. The general ended the conversation abruptly: '*Monsieur Sartre est aussi la France,*' he replied imperiously, justifying not only the protection enjoyed by the intellectual, but also the criterion on the basis of which he deserved it: *la France.*

Newspaper editors suffer from an unstoppable tendency to emulate the author of *Being and Nothingness*, and to imagine that their titles belong to the cultural, intellectual and political baggage of the societies in which they are published. Nobody doubts that *The Times* – in spite of its recent trend towards a popular rather than quality paper – continues to see itself as a symbol of England, as does *Le Monde* in France or *Frankfurter Allgemeine Zeitung* in Germany.

Meanwhile, it is difficult to find dailies or weeklies that openly express a sense of European identity. The only paper that could aspire to do so with any chance of success, because of its global vocation, is, paradoxically, a US paper: the *International Herald Tribune*; published in English, naturally enough.

Do we have such a thing as a lingua franca on our continent? The identification of a European culture as such only began with Romanisation, thanks to the massive extension of Latin as the universal language of culture. The Holy Empire was able to reinforce this linguistic identity with the much more powerful force of religious conviction. And it is this kind of fantasy, sometimes made real by the spilling of more than a little blood, that has kept us alive practically until the present.

History shows that languages are created by people but imposed by empires. Arnold Toynbee has already pointed out the fact that while in the Old Testament the proliferation of languages is shown as a torment and a divine punishment against the arrogant architects of the Tower of Babel, the first gift given to the apostles at Pentecost was the gift of tongues. The plurality of languages is still considered today to be an important part of our cultural and historical richness.

The most extreme facet of this belief is the fact that some languages, such as Gaelic and Basque, receive considerable amounts of public aid to defend themselves against the invasion of the dominant languages of their respective states. However, plurality of idioms is still an obstacle in the creation of a mass media that could bring us closer to a unitary consciousness of Europe.

Almost since the dawn of time, language, weapons and money have been the most powerful means of human communication and socialisation. In recent Europe, up to the creation of the euro, this tripod stood on US legs. If English is now the lingua franca of our continent, it is because of the worldwide globalisation process, stimulated by the USA.

The European army par excellence, NATO, is under the orders of a US general. And, until very recently, the dollar was the monetary standard most heeded by the economies of western Europe. The creation of the euro provides, for the first time, a powerful European medium of communication and will contribute to the invention and foundation of others.

The cultural unity of Europe is as evident from outside the continent as it is debatable and confused from within, even to the point that many see the US as merely a form of Europe gone adrift.

Our insistence on the diversity of our peoples cannot hinder the tendency to unify ways and customs, from fashion to food, from movies to travel. We cannot take every step in this process as a loss or an alienation. The question is to know how the media, whether multilingual or not, might contribute to the construction of Europe, not only as a confederation of interests but also as a conjunction of feelings.

Recent attempts to build a European press are not distinguished by success. The failure of the *European* is not as sad, however, as the 'success' of the tedious and bureaucratically protected Euronews TV channel, successfully boring the public in half a dozen languages.

But the illusion of difference, of the diversity of local or regional publications, serving minority or partial identities, is gradually being eroded by the concentration of media ownership. The fragmentation of the media does not necessarily mean plurality. The two main magazine groups working in Spain are French and German. The leading economic daily in Paris is owned by Pearson, as it is in Madrid. The most avidly chauvinistic media are protected and sponsored by multinational conglomerates which, in turn, are often subservient in the face of the excesses of local or national powers. Government interests have no better ally than the supposedly neutral or apolitical attitudes of foreign-owned newspapers, radio or television channels.

Beyond the print and audio-visual media, it is the likely evolution of the so-called global information society, with digital processes and the advance of the Internet and other networks, that will transform our current communicational habits.

In the digital society, the supremacy of English is absolute. Nicholas Negroponte, the guru of the cybernetic word, predicts that a functional command of the English language will be indispensable to function on the Net. He compares it to the needs of pilots and air-traffic controllers, who use English as their work language, although in the cockpit they speak their mother tongue. Once again, it seems obvious that the worldwide expansion of English as a lingua franca is inevitable.

Inevitably, this will affect the sensibilities and feelings of the identity of Europeans. However, the language with the most speakers in Europe is German. The conclusion is that most European citizens will need, usually, to speak at least two tongues and, in many cases, three. In short, cultural diversity is an intrinsic part of European unitary identity. It is what Edgar Morin defined as 'Unitas multiplex' in his book *Penser l'Europe* (Think Europe). This plurality will be enhanced, and confused, by the entry of an increasing number of people belonging to different ethnic groups, religions and cultures. In a world where racism, xenophobia and even fascism are growing under the flag of nationalism, the media have a responsibility to promote understanding.

Paradoxically, all this diversity tends to become homogenised as a result of the abrasive extension of English and the powerful processes of business concentration in the media section. Only a few years from now, less than a dozen companies – British, German, French and, maybe, Italian – will control the majority of the content of communications in the European continent. Smaller, but more advanced countries, such as The Netherlands, may be able to defend themselves in this territory. But many of the so-called national cultures and local identities will submit their balance sheets to foreign boards of directors.

Yet, paradoxically, this will be the only way of protecting ourselves (if we want to be protected) against the US invasion. The plurality of Europe, its multiplicity and diversity, which we all praise and promote, will finally be left in very few, and rather similar, hands. As the French writer Sami Nair points out: 'Western civilisation has become global and thus cultures are local . . . unifying divides; trying to include everybody expels any individual; globalisation comes back to nationalisms . . .' This is the new European culture that the media must deal with. ❏

Juan Luís Cebrián is publisher of El País, Spain. *This article appears courtesy of* New Perspectives Quarterly

SHADA ISLAM

Without the gates

I applied for my Belgian/European Union identity card and passport 11 years ago. I remember the day well: six months pregnant at the time, I had stood all morning in a long queue at the German embassy in Brussels, waiting for three hours while a surly diplomat pondered suspiciously over my visa request to attend an EU summit in Hanover. The questions came fast and furious. Was I going to stay on in Germany to become a guest worker? Did I have family in the country? Could I prove I was a journalist and that I had entered Belgium legally? Did I have a permit to work?

Exhausted and angered by this experience – and similarly painful earlier ones at the French, British, Swiss and Italian embassies – I knew it was time to take some key decisions. Fortress Europe left me little choice. I could become a cherished EU insider, free to travel effortlessly across borders. Or I could remain an unwanted outsider, a 'foreigner' who – before the Schengen agreement on the elimination of EU-wide border controls came into force – required a visa to set foot outside his or her country of legal residence.

Acquiring EU documents has certainly made life that much easier. Red tape and bureaucracy are easier to deal with. But something vital is missing. True, I possess Belgian and European identity cards, yet after spending 25 years studying, working and living in Europe, I am still struggling to acquire a real European identity.

Partly, it is my fault. My connections with my country of origin remain strong, overriding the network of ties, both professional and personal, established in my adopted country. I cling to my religion, culture and language, and I am determined that my children – half Asian, half European – should know as much about their faraway motherland as they do about their father's Europe.

But Europe is in my heart and soul. I speak at least two European languages better than my mother tongue. I'd rather wear western clothes than the more elegant Asian fashions that I now keep for special occasions. When it comes to food, it's a tie between curry, paella and pasta.

Most important, I am inspired by the EU's search for peaceful integration and co-operation among neighbours, not the permanent state of war and tension that characterises so many Asian nations. And I am not alone. Across Europe, millions of Asians, Africans, Arabs and others have made Europe their permanent home while maintaining strong links with the countries and families they left behind. We have a unique ability to live simultaneously in two parallel worlds – that of our ancestors and the new one in which our children are being born.

Look around you: Europe is a vibrant mixture of cultures, ethnic groups and religions. It is diverse, multicultural and multicoloured. But many Europeans, closing their eyes to the epic changes taking place in their communities, refuse to come to terms with the new minorities living in their midst. Certainly many European politicians and policymakers would like to pretend that Europe was otherwise.

Diversity appears to pose less problems elsewhere. My cousins in New Jersey carry their 'Asian-America' identity like a badge of honour. Younger relatives in London are funky British Asians, eager to talk about the latest Asian bands and clubs in the city. Across the rest of Europe, however, moves to recognise ethnic minorities as an integral part of mainstream Europe remain patchy.

At best we remain exotic, foreign, objects of curiosity. At worst, there are the daily encounters with discrimination, harassment and racism. Europe, through a myriad of ways, makes it clear that many of its ethnic minority citizens – not to mention the desperate asylum seekers and economic refugees trying to get in – are unwanted. The EU is generally a rich and prosperous place, free of the wars and famines that routinely devastate less fortunate parts of the globe. The Europe I see around me often engulfs me with sadness and apprehension.

EU politicians who raged against the entry into the Austrian coalition last year of the far-right Freedom Party (FPÖ) are themselves erecting new barriers to prevent refugees and asylum seekers from entering their own countries. Talking tough on immigration wins votes. Preaching tolerance is for bleeding hearts and wimps. This is not a Europe I want to be part of.

The rhetoric may change now that it is clear that the EU needs all kinds of skilled immigrants to run its information technology industries, pay for pension schemes for a rapidly ageing population and generally keep the European economy powering ahead. Already Germany is finding it difficult to attract Asian computer experts who fear an encounter with the country's anti-foreigner right-wing groups.

Perhaps one day I will feel genuinely European, proud to belong to a new, tolerant and diverse Europe. For the moment, however, I'm content to watch from the sidelines. ❑

Shada Islam *is a Brussels-based journalist and broadcaster*

SALIL TRIPATHI

Put out less flags

**Could the despised euro actually provide the sense of identity
so long sought by the European Union?**

Newly independent countries feel the need to assert their identity
with a bunch of standard icons: a flag, an anthem, a passport and
their own currency.

But 11 of the 15 European nations that make up the EU are about
to surrender perhaps the most important of these: their currency. By
giving up their currencies, they demonstrate their conviction that their
economic interests are intertwined and enmeshed so closely that they
can give up their right to spend and save the way they want.

Britain stands apart from all this. It can't give up the comforting
certainty of sterling, once the international currency of reserve, for
the unreliable and slippery euro, anxious for the standing of the dollar
without having earned it. British doubters say its economic cycle is more
closely aligned to the US's, and not Europe's (a point the International
Monetary Fund recently endorsed); that five vaguely worded financial
tests have to be met (Britain meets most of them, in any case); and that
the euro is too weak.

But at heart the issue is about cultural identity. Surrendering the
pound puts the seal on the decline of Britain as a major power since the
end of World War II. The colonies are gone, the Suez crisis showed that
old gunboat diplomacy wouldn't work, de Gaulle made Britain wait
before it could join the ECM and, in bombing Kosovo and Baghdad,
Britain is often seen as the sole cheerleader for US foreign policy
interests.

Domestically, too, British icons are under threat. Chicken tikka
masala, and not fish and chips, is the country's favourite dish; British
beef is no longer safe; telephone booths are disappearing; and foreigners
are running most of the country's household brands. Little wonder that

Ffion Hague, wife of the Conservative Party leader, wore a gold pendant made of the symbol of the pound at the Conservative Party conference.

But the world is losing patience and foreign investors are grumbling. Japanese companies have asked their British subsidiaries to quote prices in euros not pounds and are threatening to ship their plants to the continent if Britain continues to let its heart rule its head. There are strong economic arguments for Britain to join euroland; these include reduced exchange risks, lower prices, more efficient markets and prudent fiscal policies. Its backers see the euro as the logical follow-up to the common market allowing for free movement of goods, capital and services. It will, hope its advocates, strengthen Europe's economic and political identity as the euro becomes a counterweight to the influence of the US dollar, which the Japanese yen has signally failed to do. It may also, of course, force countries to pursue economic policies that hurt their populations.

But while the world of Alan Greenspan, chairman of the US Federal Reserve, can move markets, however much Wim Duisenberg, Dutch governor of the European Central Bank (ECB), might try to emulate him, he lacks the backing of an equivalent political authority. The result? A currency that bobs up and down like a cork on the ocean, earning Mr Duisenberg the undeserved epithet from Britain's jingoistic tabloid press, Wim the Dim.

If they wish it to succeed, the supporters of the euro will ultimately have to be candid and proclaim that the new currency is as much about political union as about the undoubtedly attractive economic arguments. As Thomas Risse of the European University Institute argues, 'The visions about European order which give political meaning to European Monetary Union need to be understood in the framework of identity politics.'

Politicians want to avoid that debate. At its best, europhiles view the new European identity as one based on Kantian 'pacific federation', eurosceptics point out the underlying Hegelian disdain for the masses in the manner of its creation. British eurosceptics correctly understand the political import. John Redwood of the Conservative Party once claimed: 'Abolish the pound and you abolish Britain. You make a decisive move towards a country called Europe governed from Brussels and Frankfurt . . . the intention is the establishment of a new country.' A eurosceptic website puts it more bluntly: 'If we have the euro, our gold and foreign currency reserves will be pooled and the unelected and unsackable

European central bankers will have total overall control. We will be taxed extremely heavily to support Ireland, Spain, Portugal and Greece.'

These attitudes stem from the continued perception of Europe as the other in British discourse. British identification with its own icons is so potent that it outweighs affection for European symbols: the British Crown represents the island's independence from Rome and the Continent: the Mother of Parliaments symbolises the superiority of the will of the people over the will of the ruler. As Risse has argued: 'It is not surprising that British objections against transferring sovereignty to European supranational institutions are usually justified on grounds of lacking democratic – meaning parliamentary – accountability. That this argument has more to do with collective national identity than with concerns about democracy in Europe becomes obvious when the same British leaders routinely object to strengthening the powers of the European Parliament.'

Contrast that with Germany. It probably doesn't need the euro, yet is enthusiastic about it. Thomas Mann once wrote: 'We do not want a German Europe, but a European Germany.' The Maastricht Treaty and European Monetary Union were efforts to contain a resurgent Germany; when the Bundesbank and the Deutschmark became the two spectacular success stories of post-war West Germany, post-Wall Germany was willing to surrender those successes to assure its European neighbours that its militaristic past was now buried deep. Writing about Indonesia, Ben Anderson termed nations 'imagined communities'. The European Union has been an imagined community for a long time. The common currency – and the elimination of former currencies – is the strongest manifestation yet of the region's collective desire to embrace a broader and firmer identity. While the markets don't care about flags, anthems and passports, they do care about currencies. And markets trust currencies that have the backing of a stable political power. European leaders have avoided this discussion; debate on political union remains censored out. The British will have its choice probably by 2003. Whatever decision they then take, it would at least be based on the consent of the electorate. If the euro is not to suffer a backlash, the ECB will have to be given considerable autonomy. Otherwise, the currency will collapse and with it, the hopes of a common European identity. ❏

Salil Tripathi *is a London-based writer and a regular contributor to* Index

IGNACIO URRUTIA

Afraid of silence

A sustained campaign of violence against journalists and academics has led critics of the Basque separatist army, ETA, to talk of fascism

On 7 May last year, journalist José Luis López de Lacalle, 62, followed his usual weekend rituals in Andoain. After browsing the headlines over the Internet, he bought eight daily papers and drank some coffee in a nearby café. On his way home he was shot dead by members of the Euzkadi Ta Askatasuna (ETA).

López de Lacalle had led a very full life. During the Franco dictatorship, he was imprisoned for his sympathy with Partido Comunista de España. He was a founder of the Basque branch of Izquierda Unida/Ezker Batua (United Left), and a member of the trade union Comisiones Obreras. Always an original thinker, his recent activities included a regular column in the newspaper *El Mundo*, and active membership of Foro de Ermua, a citizens' group established in February 1998 to find alternative solutions to a war that has lasted over 30 years.

So why did ETA kill López de Lacalle? Shortly after the killing, a communiqué from the organisation explained: 'In the guise of an opinion maker, he had called for the detention, torture and death of Basque citizens under the fascist slogan "Let's go for them" and the hypocritical slogan "Enough is enough!" (ya basta!) . . . (Foro de Ermua) supports the oppression of the Basque Country and the perpetuation of the conflict, even when ETA unilaterally suspends action.'

So, in principle, ETA justified the killing because of opinions that López de Lacalle freely expressed which, it goes without saying, did not include any endorsement of torture or murder. And, secondly, with this document, ETA officially declared open war on Foro de Ermua and its members.

Foro de Ermua was established after the kidnap and murder of Miguel Angel Blanco in Ermua, in July 1997. ETA had announced that the conservative town councillor would be killed within 48 hours unless all ETA prisoners held on Spanish territory were transferred to prisons in the Basque Country. Hundreds of thousands of people, both Basque and non-Basque, took to the streets as a result, demanding Blanco's release.

Foro de Ermua maintains that this 'civil explosion' marked a new phase in the fight against what it considers fascism in the Basque Country, which goes far beyond initiatives by peace groups such as Gesto por la Paz. Where Gesto por la Paz uses silent marches as a means of expressing grief and public rejection of ETA violence, Foro de Ermua encourages spontaneous, emotionally charged demonstrations in which thousands clamour against the climate of terrorism. One of Foro's chief slogans paraphrased the words of Basque poet Blas de Otero: 'Let's go for them, with Peace and the Word'.

Foro de Ermua has been highly critical of Basque nationalism since its foundation, but particularly after October 1998 when the ruling Partido Popolar formed a coalition government in the autonomous Basque region with Euskal Herria, ETA's political wing. It became more critical still at the end of the 16-month truce, which highlighted the coalition's total inability to obtain a permanent ceasefire. Since the mid-1990s, ETA has embraced what it calls the 'strategy of the socialisation of pain'. The idea is simple but sinister: 'Our prisoners and their families are suffering, while a lot of people in the Basque Country lead normal lives. Let us socialise pain so that everyone in the Basque country suffers as we do.'

This strategy has informed all ETA's recent activities. 'Legitimate' targets are no longer solely the military or members of the various police forces. Anyone can be a victim. In practice, the new 'priority' targets include local politicians, small entrepreneurs who do not pay the 'revolutionary tax' that supports ETA's armed struggle, and those who publicly criticise ETA's methods.

ETA attacks on journalists and academics have multiplied in recent months. Letter bombs have been sent to popular radio journalists Luis del Olmo and Carlos Herrera, another exploded in the Barcelona office of the newspaper *El Mundo*, while another, targeting Jesús María Zuloaga of *La Razón*, failed to cause any damage. As did bombs sent to Aurora Intxausti and Juan Palomo, reporters for Antena 3 TV and *El País* respectively.

Last November the Basque magazine *Ardi Beltza* (The Black Sheep) published a video entitled *The Business of Lying*, which accused journalists of being 'media loudspeakers for the ministry of home affairs'. The reporters singled out in the video work across the media spectrum: for the best-selling Basque newspaper *El Correo*, *El Mundo*, Radio Nacional de España, Onda Cero and CNN+. Among the journalists cited are the above-mentioned Luis del Olmo – and the deceased López de Lacalle. The director of *Ardi Beltza*, Pepe Rei, who had already been accused of collaboration with ETA, is now awaiting trial. According to Reporters sans Frontières, around 100 journalists live under some protection from the ETA death squads in Spain, most in the Basque Country itself. Ten have gone into exile.

Intellectuals are hardly in a better position. Mikel Azurmendi, a member of ETA in the 1960s and teacher at the University of the Basque Country (UPV/EHU), recently abandoned his homeland and accepted a job at a US university. Ernest Lluch, a Catalan who worked to improve relations between nationalists and constitutionalists, was assassinated by ETA in Barcelona last November. After a recent failed bomb attempt against lecturer Edurne Uriarte, UPV/EHU organised a public act of defiance.

Spain 1996: ETA's army of liberation.
Credit: © Harry Gruyaert

The principal warned against the ETA dictatorship of terror.

'I am afraid. Afraid of the suppression of freedom of thought; afraid we may succumb to the threat of terror; I am afraid of silence; afraid that, fed up with constant intimidation, we will keep silent; afraid of this situation being prelude to the end of democracy in the Basque Country. This democracy which, I insist, is in serious danger, could disappear, or go on conditioned by terror.' ❑

Ignacio Urrutia has been a volunteer for Gesto por la Paz (Association for Peace in the Basque Country) for more than ten years

IRENA MARYNIAK

Flight to Strasbourg

Along with Poland and the Czech Republic, Hungary is in the first wave of central European countries to be admitted into the EU. It hopes to fulfil the 'Copenhagen Criteria' (democratic rights and a functioning market economy) in the next two or three years. But concerns about its treatment of its Roma minority may upset these plans

In July 2000, 52 Hungarian Roma applied for political asylum in Strasbourg after being subjected to violence, evictions, death threats and vandalism over a period of three years. In that time they had filed 15 complaints with the Hungarian authorities, none of which generated a response

October 1997 *Zamoly, Hungary. One of six houses where Roma families have lived since 1985 is severely damaged in a storm. Mayor moves all Gypsies to an auditorium in the Cultural Centre and has the houses bulldozed*
March 1999 *Mayor has electricity, water and heating cut in the Cultural Centre. Vandals attack the centre at night. Windows are broken and children injured. Four further attacks follow*
July 1999 *Gypsies moved to Cultural Centre in Budapest. Restrictions on their freedom of movement imposed*
August 1999 *Families returned to Zamoly and lodged in wooden houses. Threats follow. At 11.30pm on 28 August, three skinheads armed with baseball bats and knuckledusters*

arrive threatening to evict the families. A fight follows. Police are informed but do not react. A skinhead is wounded and taken to hospital. He dies the following day
October 1999 *Arson attack on Roma houses. Further attacks follow. Police find a bomb in the nearby village of Csakvar apparently intended to destroy what is left of the Gypsies' homes. Case not pursued*
November 1999 *Roma move to Budapest. Two armed men ransack their accommodation. Police do not pursue the case*
April 2000 *Families move to Csor. Harassment continues*
July 2000 *Roma leave for Strasbourg*

Roma in Hungary, 1997: 'masters of play'. Credit: Sean Sprague / Panos Pictures

The European Parliament in Strasbourg stands like a grounded UFO merged with an amphitheatre, backing on to a hushed, blowy river which courses neatly between it, the European Court of Human Rights and the Council of Europe. Midweek the area is deserted and closed to visitors, though glossy promotion leaflets are available from jaded security guards. A few miles away in the altogether livelier suburb of Koenigshoffen, six Hungarian Roma families wait in a disused bath-house with ill-disguised sanitation problems for a response to an asylum application which is making French migration officials squirm. They have been waiting seven months. Another four families from the same group are holed up in an isolated former *lycée* south-east of the city. The Office for the Protection of Refugees (Ofpra) has been called upon to give an urgent response, but so far the only reaction has been the swift denial of a misleading and provocative report in the biggest Hungarian daily *Nepszabadsag* that some members of the group had been recognised as political refugees. The Gypsies have also lodged a complaint with the European Court of Human Rights against the Hungarian state, on the grounds of severe discrimination and inadequate protection from a series of violent assaults, evictions and arson.

Hungary is expecting to be among the first central European countries to be admitted into the EU, and hopes to fulfil the 'Copenhagen Criteria' (democratic rights and a functioning market economy) in the next two or three years. But the story told by the people from Zamoly, a village 70km outside Budapest, has brought everyone up short. The evidence being what it is, to refuse them refugee status would make a mockery of European declarations on the primacy of human and minority rights. It would also be a signal to other candidates for European entry that discriminatory policies against Roma can be pursed with impunity. But to grant political asylum would be to acknowledge that an ethnic minority is being persecuted in a 'near term' accession country, with an EU-approved minorities law. The expansion process might have to be put on hold and extremists in Hungary and other parts of central Europe would have a field day. See where the money we pumped into market reform, democratisation and all these unsavoury minorities has got us? A humiliating rap over the knuckles and exclusion from the rich man's club.

In Hungary, the 600,000-strong Roma community is 75 per cent unemployed. About 100,000 people live in isolated camps with no electricity, gas, telephone, sewerage or road access. Food poisoning, TB, hepatitis B and infant mortality are rife, and life expectancy is 15 years lower than the Hungarian average. Before 1989, over 80 per cent of Gypsies were in work, but privatisation and reform left them on the periphery of the labour market. With few skills and a high level of illiteracy they have never recovered. Only one-third of Roma children go to secondary schools; many begin their education in schools for the mentally disabled. 'The great majority of Gypsy children in these schools have no mental handicap,' Hungarian Minorities Ombudsman, Jeno Kaltenbach, has reported. 'From the age of six their fate is sealed. They are doomed to be under-educated and unemployed.' An investigation found that in the Zamoly area 94 per cent of children in special schools are Roma. All this chills, particularly in the context of Lucien Israel's remarks on insanity and exclusion in his *Initiation à la Psychiatrie* (Paris, Masson, 1995): 'Mental patients represent a minority against which racial hate manifests itself. A mental patient represents evil . . . a scapegoat proving to the good man that the evil is not in him.'

Bad and mad is what everyone would like the Roma to be. They live by an unfamiliar system of order, another code of manners, different rules. They bellow, they leave a mess, they are masters of play. The Czech government recently acknowledged that 75 per cent of children relegated to special schools for the mentally retarded are Gypsy; a similar policy exists in Slovakia where skinhead violence against Roma is routine. Their exclusion from central European restaurants, discos, swimming pools, even shops, is the norm. Hungary's media likes to objectify Gypsies into layabouts with nefarious anti-values: sinful, slothful, adulterous, avaricious, barbaric. Roma represent the antithesis of Christendom's image of man the maker – doomed since the Fall to toil for a living – or indeed of the socialist idea of a working humanity in control of the means of production. 'The image of the Gypsy is closely connected to society's self-image,' Romany activist Aladar Horvath says. '81 per cent of Hungarians say Roma don't like to work; 87 per cent say they have lighter morals.'

This kind of ethnic bigotry isn't exclusive to former communist countries. Much as the EU likes to act as finger-wagging tutor to states on its periphery, it has shown remarkable reluctance to examine its own record of private citizens' initiatives against Roma over the past decade: mob violence; armed brigades preventing refugees from entering France

and Germany; lethal bomb attacks; road blockades. Last May, in Italy,
where Gypsies live in segregated, squalid settlements, the mayor of
Cernusco sul Naviglio, in the province of Milan, offered to pay 5 million
Italian lire (cUS$2,500) to anyone willing to spray manure on a Roma
camp. While the EU was developing its ethical and practical objectives
– a democratic, knowledge-based polity, high productivity, stability,
competitiveness, and perfect labour mobility for the laptop literate – the
Roma, as ever, never got a look-in. And yet Gypsies have been in Europe
since the 14th century. Half a million disappeared in World War II, but it
took the UN 50 years to take an interest and prepare a report that called
for European states to redouble efforts to protect their fundamental
rights. The author of the report, Louis Joinet, called it 'one of the most
delicate issues the subcommission had to address in the past 20 years'.

Rhetoric on citizens' dignity and the rule of law notwithstanding,
the EU has put macro-economics before human rights in its dealings
with the accession states. And the Zamoly Gypsies are calling everyone's
bluff. 'What we have done has enraged the Hungarian government,'
Jozsef Krasznai, spokesman for the Zamoly Roma said. 'But we wanted
to draw attention to what is happening . . . The situation of Roma
people in Hungary has never been as bad. Complaints to the police
about persecution and harassment are either filed away or rejected as
unsuitable for investigation. Every year about 3,000 Roma leave the
country but nobody wants to address this . . . We are engaged in a
battle against poverty. Its level is higher than people can bear, and if
this goes on it will be very hard to control. Minorities, the poor and
the unemployed will flood West European countries.'

This is not what austere, elegant, affluent Strasbourg wants to hear:
its humanitarian conscience has been stirred enough over the years.
Gliding, ecologically friendly trams packed with brash migrant workers?
It hardens the heart and turns that inhibited European stomach. The
issue of migration has featured little in the French national press in
recent months: a precautionary lid has been kept on debate about the
prospect of free movement after enlargement. It touches a raw nerve
and brings on barely suppressed panic about tidal waves of impoverished
'destabilising elements' threatening living standards, undercutting the job
market, provoking crime, bringing mayhem. It is a fear that has already
brought significant electoral gain to the xenophobic right in Austria and,
more recently, in Belgium.

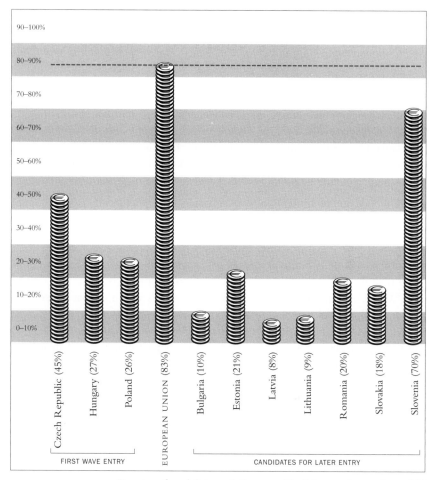

Percentage of people living on half or more of the EU average income. Source: EU

Annual migration to Europe is estimated at 800,000 including, it is said, irregular migrants from such places as Iraq, Iran, Turkey or China – the sort who suffocate in lorries or drown in the Adriatic after risking the Sarajevo route to Europe. But who knows? Half a million are thought to have made it in the first ten months of last year. British Home Secretary Jack Straw recently initiated measures towards a common asylum system in Europe to make sure it doesn't happen again.

But what about the people who in three, five, even ten years' time might come in legally, from within a fully expanded EU? There are 300,000 Roma in the Czech Republic; 500,000 in Slovakia; but nearly 3 million in Romania . . . How ever could we cope?

Traditional European perceptions of progress have been about settlement, growth, territorial expansion and resettlement. The assumption that a sedentary life is more 'advanced' than an itinerant one, that impoverished pastoral communities 'progressed' to become rich agricultural communities, runs deep. Here, as Neal Ascherson writes in *Black Sea*: 'Pseudo-anthropology feeds the basic European nightmare: a terror of people who move . . . The nightmare survives as a western fear of all travelling people, of the millions pressing against Europe's gates as "asylum seekers" or "economic migrants".' The myth of 'Asiatic' barbarism, that idea that the East and its people are unpredictable, uncontrollable, sometimes hostile and always inferior, underlies nineteenth-century Austrian chancellor Klemens Metternich's quip that Asia began behind the fence of his Viennese garden, and the first West German chancellor Konrad Adenauer's warning that 'Asia stands on the Elbe'.

The memory of sentiments like these is scarcely reassuring to central European states, anxious to assert their participation in Europe's historical and cultural development. And the tradition of West European exclusiveness or its paranoia is being projected internally, in central Europe, on to those deemed to be outside the process of defining identity and acquiring wealth: the 'non-Europeans'. The Roma have their origins outside Europe, the argument runs, they cannot be fully fledged members of the community, they are maladjusted by nature. And even if most are well settled and don't light bonfires in the middle of the living room or keep pigs in the bathtub as they've been reputed to do in the past, they are still tricksters who play the system and have no contribution to make to the political debate.

Viewed as an underclass seeking its fortune outside the mainstream, and with the additional stigma of roots in India, Gypsies are outcast on the grounds of both poverty and race. In addition, the issue of resources needed to improve their living standards in countries where governments hardly have sufficient budgets to provide for their majority populations is increasing animosity and giving extremists their chance. In the Hungarian press, dozens of articles have appeared claiming that the

Zamoly group left Hungary to squeeze benefits out of the French system, discredit their country and escape the law. There has been talk for months of the extradition from France of two women suspected of involvement in the death of a skinhead who participated in one of the attacks against the community. No action has been taken. But in the media, the issue of migration itself is now being equated with crime.

'Most people feel that what the Gypsies did was unpatriotic, typical and exploitative,' Ferenc Koszeg, president of the Hungarian Helsinki Committee, says. 'This feeds public hostility to the notion of affirmative action. There is a feeling that Gypsies claim rights without fulfilling their duties, while the poor in the majority lose out. It's similar to initial public reaction to the Black Civil Rights Movement in the US.' Polls suggest that 80 per cent of Hungarians feel that the Zamoly Roma should stay away. And who is to say whether other central European states might not be tempted to think in terms of encouraging migration as a way of 'cleansing' themselves of a minority perceived as a social and economic burden?

Clearly, if they were returned, the Zamoly group would find themselves in a rougher environment than ever. But will a Europe where the right blames migrants for a crisis of social polarisation, where only the technologically skilled are deserving, where bumpkins are relegated to the sticks, and aliens to filthy, squalid camps, want to accept them and set a precedent that might encourage other impoverished outcasts to come?

'The more affluent and stable you are, the more fearful you become,' says psychiatrist Georges Federmann, spokesman for the Support Committee for the Zamoly Roma in Strasbourg. 'Our society fosters a fantasy of inertia, the fixed, the eternal, of perfect health. Stability means ritual, it has turned secularism dogmatic. If the middle classes do not bring the marginalised into the centre they will pave the way to totalitarianism, a slow-motion fascism. That's effectively what we're beginning to see in the West.'

Irena Maryniak in Strasbourg

Henrietta's story

'It's disgusting that while I, and many like me, build our houses from
salaries we earn and work we do, there are those who do so thanks to their
talent for "making babies"'—*Jozsef Takacs, mayor of Zamoly, January 2000*
'Most Gypsies are criminals'—*Dezso Csete, mayor of Csor, May 2000*

Henrietta is 26. 'We left Hungary because of the attacks. We were
attacked in Zámoly, and in Csór and in Budapest. The scar on my
arm is where I fell on broken glass. When they smashed the windows,
my baby was in a pram just underneath. I dragged it away but fell myself.
It was dark. I managed to slash my wrist, too, and got taken to hospital.

'We were fine with the villagers at first. People gave us work on
farms and in the fields. Sometimes they invited us to weddings to wash
dishes. But after the mayor decided to pull down our houses things got
bad. He said our homes weren't fit to live in and gave us half an hour
to take what we needed before the bulldozers came. We couldn't believe
it. But it happened. Then we were put in the Cultural Centre and – you
can't imagine what it was like – all these people who'd been our friends
started to hate us. They wouldn't even say hello, though they saw we
were clean and the yard was in order and the kids went to school and
kindergarten. They said we'd ruin the Cultural Centre and we shouldn't
be staying there because there was nowhere to hold parties for the
children and pensioners' meetings.

'Then the mayor cut the water, the electricity supply and the heating.
I caught cold and had to go to hospital with my daughter. Her life
was in danger. Many of the children were taken to hospital. There
were salmonella and things. You can imagine what it was like using the
bathroom. I told the mayor that he should let us use his. There was no
excrement around the house or in the yard though, and the children
didn't pee there either. Later, though, the kids did have to use the yard,
and we took shovels and covered it all up with earth.

'We had to carry water about a kilometre and did the laundry by
hand in winter. Later, the electricity, water supply and heating were
restored. We were lucky because there was a gas-stove so we could warm
the water. Then people started breaking the windows. The children
couldn't go to school and we didn't dare go shopping. We kept the
spades and hoes inside. At Christmas, they smashed the windows and

threw bottles of petrol into the house. Then the villagers heard we'd got building plots at the end of the village and wooden houses were being built there and they threatened to burn them down. They said things like: "We'll have you out within a day." And the houses *were* set on fire, and we lost everything we had. Then we moved to Budapest and got attacked. They had firearms – the children might have been shot. Then we went back to Csór and the attacks started again. That was when we decided to leave the country.

'There were two families who couldn't afford to come. It was bad having to leave them behind. We were afraid they'd be got at and hurt. We didn't dare tell the two bus drivers that we intended to stay in France. But when they realised that we weren't going back, they weren't surprised. I think they'd suspected it.

'People are nicer here, and we're treated like human beings. We haven't experienced any hatred. And even if there are people like that, they don't show their feelings openly. But we don't know of any. We have to adapt, attune ourselves. Our children know more than we do: they're learning the language, they go to school. They're beginning to calm down, and they have everything they need. Some local kids don't acknowledge them and there have been fights. One of the problems is that they can't make themselves understood in French. I use my hands to express what I want, but not many words. . . . But kids will learn easily.

'We need peace. I think it's the most important thing. A life without that feeling of dread would be enough. And not to live crammed in tiny rooms. The problem is that we lived together in the Cultural Centre, then in Budapest, then in Csór. Now we're all together again. We get on fine, there are no rows, no fights, we're all right. It's just that we'd all like to live separately, independently.

'In Hungary they scared us so much. That fire . . . one of the kids got trapped. The worst thing was the burning houses. None of the neighbours came to help. It's as if they were glad . . . And in Budapest those people came and threatened us and shot everywhere. We didn't know where to hide. I didn't know which child to grab . . . And in the fire I didn't know what to save. I went for the kids . . . The neighbours didn't do anything. It hurt me to see how those decent people got to hate us. And to make us feel we're Gypsies.' ❑

Interview by **Irena Maryniak**. *Translated by Istvan Fenyvesi*

FLASHPOINTS

Art of noise

The curious thing about bombs, and especially bombs that have been laid to destroy a particular dissenting voice, is that they tend to draw more attention than the sound they set out to stifle. In states of war this makes little or no difference, for the symphony of bombs is the sound of the day and any small silence that swells out to occupy the vacuum between detonations counts for little in the grander narrative of explosive discourse: it's just a hiccup in the supply chain of noise.

In states of peace that border on war, bombs have very different roles to play. In Italy, during the 1970s, bloody explosions were orchestrated in public spaces by the intelligence services to fuel a 'strategy of tension', whereby popular opinion was shepherded towards the government-held centre out of a manufactured fear of the extreme left or right. A cruder version of the same tactic appears to have been used by ex-KGB agents on the residents of apartment buildings in Moscow and Buinaksk in September 1999 as a means of turning Vladimir Putin's plans for a second Chechen War into a presidential vote-winner. Over 250 Russians died, but Putin got his war and he got his majority.

The bomb 'options' for terrorist organisations are not as clear-cut as they might appear, at least in democracies. However polished the supply chain, a commander must judge to the very split second just how much blood and disruption the public can stomach before the tactic of using bombs to erode popular confidence in a government results in the opposite. When that position is reached, the continuation of bombing can only be construed as an exercise in malice, or a display of embittered weakness; in short, a waste of noise. Every explosion only serves to hammer deeper the public's resolve to say 'no' to a political settlement founded on fear. It is for this reason, perhaps, that journalists in the West are only rarely singled out for 'revolutionary justice'.

But this is changing; the bombs are back with a vengeance that seems specifically bent upon silencing media. In recent weeks there have been several well publicised attacks on news outlets and journalists in Zimbabwe, Britain and Spain and all, in different ways, serve to highlight the desperation of those who must have planted the devices.

On 27 January information minister Jonathan Moyo told the Zimbabwe Broadcasting Corporation that the state would 'silence' the *Daily News*, Harare's best-selling independent newspaper, after it published wide-ranging allegations of corruption and mismanagement against president Robert Mugabe's government. A little over 24 hours later, four bomb explosions caused damage estimated at US$2m to the newspaper's printing machinery. Sources close to the subsequent investigation told the *Zimbabwe Independent* that either a TM46 or TM57 anti-tank landmine was used in the bombing, adding credence to the popular view that the state was behind the attack.

On 4 March dissident republicans of the Real IRA, which opposes the Good Friday Peace Agreement in Northern Ireland, planted 20lb of high explosive in a taxi outside the BBC TV Centre, in London's White City district. No one was seriously injured in the attack, which appears to have been a reprisal for an award-winning *Panorama* documentary about the Real IRA's responsibility for the Omagh bombing in 1998, and the strange reluctance of the Royal Ulster Constabulary to arrest anyone for it. The special irony, however, was that the investigative programme that had invited such a surprising homage is currently clinging to the late Sunday schedules by the skin of its teeth, the victim of a viewer downturn.

In both Zimbabwe and Britain, the blasts showed up the perpetrators for the clumsy, potentially murderous bullies they are. Indeed, the Harare explosion triggered a backlash against the Mugabe government, with one conservative British weekly, the *Sunday Times*, setting up a readers' fund to replace the *News'* printing facilities. The outlook in Spain is much more gloomy (see p60). Journalists have been a favoured target in a violent campaign against the state by the Basque separatist group, Euskadi ta Askatasuna (ETA). In its most recent attack on 3 March, 20 Molotov cocktails were hurled at the offices of the Basque daily *El Correo*.

Again, no one was injured then. But, on 8 March, ETA stole 1.6 tonnes of explosives and 20,000 detonators from a French warehouse, possibly in preparation for the Basque regional elections, due in May. Spanish and Basque journalists are expecting to be on the receiving end in the very near future. ❏

MG

5

A censorship chronicle incorporating information from the American Association for the Advancement of Science Human Rights Action Network (AAASHRAN), Amnesty International (AI), Article 19 (A19), Alliance of Independent Journalists (AJI), the BBC Monitoring Service Summary of World Broadcasts (SWB), Centre for Journalism in Extreme Situations (CJES), the Committee to Protect Journalists (CPJ), Canadian Journalists for Free Expression (CJFE), Glasnost Defence Foundation (GDF), Information Centre of Human Rights & Democracy Movements in China (ICHRDMC), Instituto de Prensa y Sociedad (IPYS), The UN's Integrated Regional Information Network (IRIN), the Inter-American Press Association (IAPA), the International Federation of Journalists (IFJ/FIP), Human Rights Watch (HRW), the Media Institute of Southern Africa (MISA), Network for the Defence of Independent Media in Africa (NDIMA), International PEN (PEN), Open Media Research Institute (OMRI), Pacific Islands News Association (PINA), Radio Free Europe/ Radio Liberty (RFE/RL), Reporters Sans Frontières (RSF), the World Association of Community Broadcasters (AMARC), World Association of Newspapers (WAN), the World Organisation Against Torture (OMCT) and other sources

AFGHANISTAN

Abdul Saboor Salehzai, a translator for the BBC World Service in Kabul, has been detained incommunicado since 16 December. Several months prior to his arrest, the Taliban authorities had pres-

sured the BBC to dismiss Salehzai on the grounds that he was a 'communist'. He is also accused of violating the rules that regulate those who work with foreign media, notably by failing to obtain proper authorisations for visiting journalists. (CPJ, RSF)

ALGERIA

The Banna correspondent for the daily *El Watan* narrowly escaped injury on 7 December when his car was driven off the road by a careering truck. **Abdelbaki Djabali**, who is known for his reports exposing corruption, claimed that the lorry driver had made a number of previous attempts to cause an accident. (WAN, RSF)

ANGOLA

On 12 December journalist **Rafael Marques** was denied the right to travel outside the country, despite a court order stating unequivocally that all travel restrictions had been lifted. The journalist, convicted on charges of criminal libel in March 2000 (*Index* 2/2000, 3/2000, 5/2000, 6/2000), was beneficiary of a general amnesty on 11 November. (CPJ)

ARGENTINA

On 10 November journalists **Oscar Angel Flores** and **Mario Otero** (*Index* 1/2000) were threatened by an adviser to the governor of San Luis province, Eduardo Endeiza. Flores, head of news for Radio Dimensión, and Otero, radio broadcaster and publisher of the bi-weekly *El Decameron*,

were reproached for questions they had posed to Governor Adolfo Rodríguez Saá about corruption. (Periodistas)

Journalist **Jorge Lanata**'s (*Index* 9/1991, 2/1992, 5/1997, 2/1998) television programme *Destino* was cancelled by the Telefé management after they had included it in their broadcasting schedule. Periodistas accused the station on 5 January of bowing to political pressure. (Periodistas)

AZERBAIJAN

On 8 January the independent television station DMR TV was forced to close. **Mustafa Dibirov**, president of the station, was escorted to the police station and asked to write a letter promising he would not reopen it until he received an official licence. DMR TV has repeatedly requested a licence but this has been denied. On 25 January, independent television station Mingechevir TV stopped broadcasting after a warning that continued operation without a licence would result in criminal charges. Mingechevir TV has requested an official licence but this has been denied. (CJES)

On 31 January some 100 journalists demonstrated at the State Customs Committee in protest at the shortage and high price of newsprint. Already the newspaper *Mukhalifat* has been forced to suspend publication as a result. Rauf Arifoglu, editor-in-chief of opposition paper *Yeni Musavet*, said that the crisis is a 'thinly disguised attempt . . . to shut down independent publications in Azerbaijan'. (IWPR, CJES, Journalists' Trade Union)

Zamin Gadjiev, journalist for the daily *Azadlyg*, was attacked by three men as he returned home early in February. Two held his arms behind his back while the third sprayed tear gas into his face. Gadjiev, who has written articles critical of the government, announced he was retiring from journalism some days later. (IWPR, CJES, Journalists' Trade Union)

In early February **Etibar Mansaroglu**, editor of *Etimad*, was attacked in the street, suffering cracked ribs, a broken nose and severe concussion. Less than a week later, a traffic policeman was arrested in connection with the assault. (IWPR)

On 6 February **Hamiq Ibrahim**, journalist with the daily *Echo*, was kicked and beaten by police while covering a police operation in the Yasamal district of Baku. He was released when an unknown person telephoned the police station. (Journalists' Trade Union, A19)

BANGLADESH

On 1 January a Division Bench of the High Court ruled that a *fatwa* (religious edict), forcing a married woman to contract a second marriage against her will, was unlawful. The two judges said that *fatwa* should be declared illegal 'even if it is not executed'. Fazl-ul Huq Amini, head of the Islamic Unity

Alliance, denounced the judges as 'apostates'. (*Daily Star*, BBC News Online)

On 25 January a group of masked men in the town of Feni abducted award-winning journalist **Tipu Sultan**, of the United News of Bangladesh agency, and broke both his hands and legs so badly that they may need to be amputated. Witnesses identified the attackers as cadres of Jainal Hazari, the ruling Awami League MP in the area and editor of the weekly *Hazarika*. Sultan attempted to lodge a complaint against Hazari and his supporters while in hospital in Dhaka on 28 January, but the complaint was not registered. This procedural problem has the potential to block any investigation of this incident. (RSF, *The Daily Star*, Mass-line Media Centre)

BRITAIN

In a ruling on 18 December Judge Charles Gibson said that drug laws banning Rastafarians from using and selling cannabis may be incompatible with Article 9 of the European Convention on Human Rights, which deals with freedom of religion. (*Daily Telegraph, Guardian*)

After a record number of complaints, in December the Advertising Standards Agency banned the controversial poster for Opium perfume, which features model Sophie Dahl on a bed of blue velvet, wearing nothing but diamond jewellery and a pair of gold stiletto-heeled shoes. (*Guardian*)

The Department of Trade and Industry denied claims by comedian **Mark Thomas** on his Channel 4 show, *The Mark Thomas Product*, that minister Richard Caborn ordered 'dirt' to be collected on him. Thomas had gained access to information held in government records – a right under the Data Protection Act – that included anonymous emails incriminating the minister. (*The Times, Daily Telegraph, Guardian*)

Robert Thompson and Jon Venables, reviled killers of three-year-old Jamie Bulger, were granted blanket protection from intrusion by the media of England and Wales on 9 January. Media in Scotland, Northern Ireland and other countries were exempted, leading to claims that the injunction will be ineffectual. (*Guardian*)

The Ministry of Defence has attempted to deflect claims of a cover-up, following the leak of a 1997 internal report that warned of a heightened risk of lung, lymph and brain cancer from the use of depleted uranium ammunition. The report was discredited as the 'work of a junior officer', but later reports claim a cover sheet had recommended the report for circulation to all civilian and military personnel likely to come into contact with the munitions. On 11 January Armed Forces Minister John Spellar defended the decision not to circulate the report, saying it contained a 'number of errors'. (*Guardian*)

Journalist **John Kiddy** has issued a complaint against Devon and Cornwall police chiefs for intimidation, it was reported on 15 January. Kiddy, who had made documentaries questioning the conviction of Brian Parsons for the murder of Ivy Battenin in 1987, maintains that comments by Deputy Chief Constable Keith Portlock that criminal charges had not been ruled out amounted to 'scandalous intimidation of a journalist.' (*Press Gazette*)

Former MI6 agent **Richard Tomlinson** published memoirs of his operations in Russia, under the title *The Big Breach*, despite a ban under the Official Secrets Act. MI6 accused Tomlinson of making a deal with Russian intelligence which, it believes, is intent on embarrassing its British counterparts. In a ruling on 19 January, the *Sunday Times* was given permission to serialise extracts from the book since the publication in Russia made it impossible for the government to prevent revelations reaching the public domain. On 29 January a Scottish publisher, Mainstream, announced plans to produce the first paperback version in the UK. (*Observer, Guardian, Daily Telegraph*)

An attempt by the *Sunday Telegraph* to use the freedom of expression clause in the Human Rights Act to side-step a breach of copyright judgment was rejected by judges, it was reported on 19 January. The paper's publication on 25 November 1999 of a minute taken by former

Liberal Democrat leader Paddy Ashdown of a Downing Street meeting has been challenged by Ashdown himself. The judge said that the Human Rights Act does not trump copyright law. (*Press Gazette*)

A report on 5 February documents the ban brought against an advert for the alco-pop Reef in which a group of women in bikinis perform an imitation of the Maori war dance the Haka. The Independent Television Commission described the advert as 'crossing the boundary between poor taste and serious offence'. (*Daily Telegraph*)

It was announced on 7 February that Woolworths has banned the new pre-teenage magazine *Mad About Boys* from its shelves; aimed at nine- to twelve-year-olds, it allegedly 'encourages them to dress inappropriately'. (*Guardian*)

On 16 February the *Guardian* announced the launch of a High Court challenge to the 1848 Treason Felony Act, which provides for a life sentence for anyone calling for the abolition of the monarchy in print. (*Guardian*)

The new Terrorism Act, which came into force on 19 February, allows ministers to extend the list of proscribed organisations to include foreign groups that organise terrorist campaigns from the UK (*Index* 4/2000). The act extends the definition of terrorism, previously an exclusively political crime, to include religious or ideological causes and 'cyber-terrorists'. (*Daily Telegraph*)

Campaign Against the Arms Trade released a list of public institutions investing in six leading arms companies in the UK on 21 February. The list includes charities such as the Leukaemia Research Fund, health trusts, educational institutions including certain colleges in Oxford and Cambridge, local authorities and the Labour Party. (Campaign Against the Arms Trade)

BURKINA FASO

On 6 December all demonstrations were banned by the government in response to student protests at the University of Ouagadougou in which a child, Flavien Nébié, was killed. (RSF)

On 8 January two journalists from the weekly newspaper founded by **Norbert Zongo,** *L'Indépendent*, were detained. **Germain Nama** and **Newton Ahmed Barry** were investigating the death of Flavien Nébié, the schoolboy killed in the demonstration on 6 December. They were first questioned and then taken to Boussé where the events that led up to Nébié's death occurred. On 9 January the journalists were released in Ouagadougou and promptly handed over to the state prosecutor a bullet they had located in a tree in Boussé which, they believe, is related to the boy's death. (RSF)

On 17 January the examining magistrate heard François Compaoré, the president's brother, testify in the **Norbert Zongo** case. On 2 February Attorney General Abdoulaye

Barry charged warrant officer Marcel Kafando with 'murder' and 'arson'. Kafando is one of six serious suspects from the presidential guard identified as taking part in the murder. (RSF)

BURMA

On 20 December **Aung Myint**, head of the information department of the National League for Democracy (NLD), was sentenced to 21 years in prison for violating the emergency law. His assistant, **Kyaw Sein Oo,** was sentenced to seven years for violating the press law. Both journalists were arrested on 14 September accused of distributing information to foreign media about the repression of the NLD. (RSF)

CHAD

On 4 December, after a complaint by the secretary-general of the government, journalist **Garondé Djarama** of *N'Djaména Hebdo* was given a six-month suspended sentence for articles about Libyan relations with Chad published on 7 November (*Index* 5/2000). The publisher of *N'Djaména Hebdo*, **Oulatar Begoto Nicolas**, was acquitted. (RSF)

On 21 December **Mickael Didama**, publisher of *Le Temps*, was detained by police after General Mahammat Ali Abdallah, nephew of President Idriss Deby, lodged a complaint for defamation following publication of an article that focused on alleged coup attempts by his the president's relatives. The article

was signed by journalist **Séverin Georges Guetta**. On 1 February Didama was given a suspended prison sentence and hefty fines and damages. (RSF)

CHILE

The arrest warrant on journalist **Alejandra Matus** (*Index* 4/1999, 6/1999) remains in place after a ruling in mid-December that the author of the banned *El libro negro de la justicia*, who lives in exile in Miami, has no further recourse to appeal. (Digital Freedom Network, IAPA, Periodistas)

Juan Pablo Cárdenas, editor of the online Primera Línea, was dismissed on 10 January because the government did not like his editorial line. Primera Línea, launched in September 2000, had uncovered scandals involving government officials. After refusing to resign, Cárdenas was dismissed by his board. (IPYS)

A previously unpublished document directly incriminating General Augusto Pinochet in the 'Caravan of Death', a helicopter flight which saw 75 suspected leftists dumped into the sea in 1973, was published by the electronic newspaper *El Mostrador* on 7 February. The presentation included a handwritten note by Pinochet, proposing ways of hiding one of the executions. (EFE)

On 12 February Hernán Gabrielli Rojas, chief of staff of the Air Force, initiated legal action against **Carlos Bau**, **Héctor Vera** and **Juan Ruz**

for violating state security law. Bau told *El Mostrador* on 8 February that Gabrielli had tortured him in September 1973 at the Cerro Moreno air force base. Vera and Ruz gave similar statements to *La Nación* and *La Tercera* two days later. Gabrielli denied the accusations. The law protects Gabrielli from slander and, because Bau's statements were repeated in the media, he is to be tried by Court of Appeals Judge Jaime Rodríguez Espoz – the same judge who upheld the case against Alejandra Matus. (IPYS)

CHINA

Falun Gong adherents continue to fall foul of the authorities in numbers too great to record here. For fully referenced information about victims of the persecution from 7 December to 7 February, visit: www.indexoncensorship.org/news/

Senior editors in Guangdong were called to an 'urgent meeting' on 12 December with the provincial publicity department and given a 'blacklist' of 11 journalists and academics whose works are not to be reproduced. The list included **Prof. He Zouxin**, an outspoken critic of Falun Gong; economist **Cao Si-yuan**, a prolific writer on bankruptcy; **Mao Yushi, Fan Gang** and historian **Prof. Liu Junning** (*Index* 3/2000); journalist and sociologist **He Qinglian** (*Index* 5/2000); the scholars **Lin Xianzhi** and **Zhu Queqin**; economist **Qin Hui**; historian **Qian Liqun**; and writer **Yu Jie**. (*South China Morning Post*)

• •

DENG XIAOPING, LI PENG, WANG ZHEN, ZHAO ZIYANG
Four men and a funeral

WANG ZHEN: Those goddam bastards! Who do they think they are, trampling on sacred ground like Tiananmen? We should send in the troops right now to grab those counter-revolutionaries. Comrade Xiaoping, what are the People's Liberation Army (PLA) for? They're not supposed to just sit around and eat. We've got to do it, or we'll never forgive ourselves. Anyone who tries to overthrow the Communist Party deserves death and no burial.

DENG XIAOPING: The elder comrades are burning with anxiety at what they see in Beijing these days: [students] lying down on railway tracks, beating, smashing and robbing; if this isn't turmoil, what is? If things continue, we could even end up under house arrest. I've concluded we should bring in the PLA and declare martial law. The aim will be to suppress the turmoil and to return things quickly to normal. This is the unshirkable duty of the Party and government. I am solemnly proposing this to the Standing Committee of the Politburo and hope you will consider it.

ZHAO ZIYANG: But Comrade Xiaoping, it will be hard for me to carry out this plan. I have difficulties with it.

DENG XIAOPING: The minority yields to the majority!

ZHAO ZIYANG: I submit to party discipline; the minority does yield to the majority.

DENG XIAOPING: The western world, especially the USA, has thrown its entire propaganda machine into agitation and has given a lot of encouragement and assistance to the so-called democrats and opposition – people who are, in fact, the scum of the nation. Some western countries use things like 'human rights' to criticise us. What they're really after is our sovereignty.

LI PENG: I strongly urge that we move immediately to clear Tiananmen Square and that we resolutely put an end to the turmoil.

DENG XIAOPING: I agree and suggest that martial law begin tonight. As we proceed with the clearing, we must explain clearly to all the citizens and students, asking them to leave. But if they refuse to leave, they will be responsible for the consequences . . . ❏

Excerpt from the 'Tiananmen Papers', a recently released transcript of conversations between Zhao Ziyang, the moderate general secretary of the Communist Party, and vice-president Wang Zhen, prime minister Li Peng and president Deng Xiaoping on the eve of the Tiananmen Square massacre

• •

Under a law enacted on 1 January, broadcasters can be taken off-air for using any language other than the official dialect of Mandarin. It will also be an offence to show billboards, advertisements and product labels with 'spelling mistakes'. (Agence France-Presse)

In a speech on 11 January to an assembly of provincial propaganda chiefs responsible for censorship, President Jiang Zemin warned official media to toe the party line and not carry material critical of government. 'The news media is the mouthpiece of the party and the people,' he said, 'and should publicise the spirit of the party central committee in a precise, clear and vivid manner.' (Agence France-Presse, Xinhua)

Huang Qi, arrested last June for placing critical articles on his www.6-4tianwang.com website (*Index* 4/2000, 5/2000), was committed for trial for subversion on 13 February in Chengdu, Sichuan Province. Huang collapsed several hours into his trial. He looked thin, was missing a tooth and had been scarred on his forehead, (Agence France-Presse, Associated Press, Reuters, BBC, CPJ)

COLOMBIA

Journalist **Alfredo Abad López** was murdered on leaving his Florencia home on 13 December. It is believed that the killing was triggered by his investigation into the murder of his colleague **Guillermo León Agudelo** two weeks previously. Abad was director of Voz de la Selva, part of the Caracol radio network, for which Agudelo also worked. (CPJ, RSF)

Winston Viracacha, Caracol TV correspondent and head of press for the department of Nariño, was abducted on 15 December, apparently by the National Liberation Army (ELN), in reprisal for his 'biased' reporting of the group's activities. (IAPA, IPYS, RSF)

The murder of journalist and humorist **Jaime Garzón** in August 1999 (*Index* 5/1999, 6/1999, 1/2000) is likely to have been carried out by paramilitaries. The disguised leader of 'La Terraza' hit squad admitted on Canal Caracol on 17 December that his group had murdered Garzón. Despite the admission, no one has yet been tried for the murder. (IPYS)

Investigations into the murder of **Carlos Lajud Catalan** in March 1993 (*Index* 5/1993, 6/1993) are concentrating on the likelihood that Bernardo Hoyos Montoya, priest and twice mayor of Barranquilla, ordered the murder. (IPYS)

It was announced on 24 January that radio journalists **Carlos Enrique Aristizabal** and **Guillermo Aguilar** were in hiding after being threatened by ELN rebels. Aristizabal previously worked on the Cali-based radio programme *Voces de Libertad*, which provided a message service for relatives of the ELN's kidnap victims. (IPYS)

Television host and journalist **Claudia Gurisatti** left the country on 30 January on the advice of the intelligence service, which uncovered a plan to assassinate her. Gurisatti had received threatening notes and calls since interviewing well-known figures in the armed conflict on her programme *La Noche*, among them the rebel group Fuerzas Armadas Revolucionarias de Colombia's (FARC) spokesperson, Raúl Reyes. A hired killer captured by the authorities confessed that his friend had been contracted by FARC to assassinate Gurisatti. (IPYS)

An attempt was made on 15 February to assassinate **Raúl Benoit**, correspondent for Univisión, the largest, Spanish-language channel in the US. Benoit was attacked in Cali by a gunman whom his two bodyguards attacked and injured. The assailant was Carlos Emilio Molina, a police officer for eight years. (RSF, Periodistas)

COSTA RICA

On 24 January the Supreme Court defeated efforts by *La Nación* journalist **Mauricio Herrera Ulloa** to overturn a lower court ruling against him in a defamation and libel case brought by diplomat Félix Przedborski. Ulloa based a series of articles in 1995 on reports of Przedborski's financial misdealings in Europe that had been published in such magazines as *Der Spiegel* and *La Libre Belgique*. (RSF)

CÔTE D'IVOIRE

On 11 January five journalists from the daily opposition newspaper *Le Patriote* were summoned by police because of suspected involvement in a failed coup attempt on 8 January. Only editor-in-chief **Sindou Meite** responded to the summons. On 13 January a number of Abidjan newspapers reported that Meite's home had been ransacked by unidentified individuals. (CPJ)

On 17 January **Mohamed Junior Ouattara**, a journalist with Agence France-Presse, was approached by a man in civilian clothes who asked his identity. Ouattara and his colleagues were then roughed up by three others, before Ouattara was handcuffed. The men later identified themselves as police officers. Ouattara was accused of involvement in the failed 8 January coup and detained at the office for counter-espionage services. He was released without charge on 22 January. (RSF)

On 10 February the printing press of Abidjan daily *Le Jour* was raided by 30 armed men and three police officers. They accused the absent administrative director, **Biamari Coulibaly**, of preparing for a coup by gathering arms and recruiting mercenaries. According to the paper's editor-in-chief, **Abdoulaye Sangare**, they threatened to kill Coulibaly if they found him. (CPJ)

CUBA

On 12 January journalists expressed support for the *Financial Times* correspondent Pascal Fletcher, who was personally condemned by President Fidel Castro on a television programme that was broadcast on the evening of 9 January. Castro accused Fletcher of publishing 'tendentious information' and objected to his use of confidential economic data in his reports. Personal information about the journalist was provided on-air. (IAPA)

Two Czechs – Ivan Pilip, a former finance minister and parliamentary deputy from the centre-right Freedom Union party, and former student leader Jan Bubenik – were arrested on the weekend of 13–14 January after meeting anti-Castro dissidents in the central province of Ciego de Avila. Antonio Femenías, director of the independent news agency Patria, and Roberto Valdivia, a journalist affiliated with Patria, met the two Czechs on 11 January. Since the meeting, both journalists have been repeatedly interrogated by state security. The two Czechs were released on 5 February and allowed to return home. (Reuters, *El País*, *Daily Telegraph*)

Jesus Joel Díaz Hernández, executive director of the independent news service Cooperativa Avilena de Periodistas Independientes, was released from prison on 18 January, having served two years of a four-year sentence for the crime of 'dangerousness'. (CPJ)

DEMOCRATIC REPUBLIC OF CONGO

Marcel Ngoyi Kyenge, secretary-general of the pro-government daily *L'Avenir*, had his home invaded by three soldiers, it was reported on 25 December. The three assailants locked up the journalist's children before splashing gasoline on the furniture and setting the room on fire. Kyenge's oldest son managed to escape and alert neighbours. According to the daily *La Tempête des Tropiques*, the soldiers left a message saying: 'Marcel Mgoyi, mind your own business, or your family will disappear. Risk of death. First warning.' A few days later, **Welo M'Peti**, a journalist with the Congolese News Agency, was abducted by four soldiers as he was returning from Kinshasa airport. He was severely beaten. (Journaliste en Danger)

On 4 January **Freddy Loseke Lisumbu** of *La Libre Afrique* (*Index*, 2/2000, 3/2000, 4/2000) and **Emile-Aimé Kakese Vinalu** of *Le Carousel* (*Index* 5/2000) and **Jean-Pierre Ekanga Mukuna** of *Le Tribune de la National*, were released, as a token of good faith, by President Laurent Kabila. (Journaliste en Danger)

The weekly *Le Flambeau* was suspended on 13 January and its editor, **Richard Ntsana**, detained for publishing an article which 'created confusion' about state institutions. (RSF)

Four armed soldiers in civilian clothes invaded the home of **Clovis Kadda**, editor of the twice-weekly *L'Alarme*, from 13 to 14 February. Visitors in the house reported that they had been robbed and prevented from leaving. The attack was apparently in connection with a published interview with **Honoré Ngbanda**, a former special security councillor to the late president Mobutu, which appeared in *Jeune Afrique Economie* and which called into question the parentage of President Joseph Kabila. (Journaliste en Danger)

A dozen members of the Rapid Intervention Police (PIR) burst into Victoria Square in Kinshasa on 16 February, detaining five newspaper vendors for selling that week's issue of *Alerte Plus*. The paper carried the headline, 'Fall-out from the assassination of Laurent-Désiré Kabila – list of 16 military officers arrested.' (Journaliste en Danger)

DJIBOUTI

Editor **Daher Ahmed Farah** of the weekly *Le Renouveau* was detained at his residence on 15 January, and the newspaper suspended, after he was charged with the 'distribution of false news and defamation'. The suspension followed a complaint by the chief of police. *Le Renouveau* is the mouthpiece of the Democrat Renewal Party, an opposition party led by Farah. (RSF)

ECUADOR

After an uprising by the indigenous population from 21 January to 6 February, the government announced a national state of emergency in which media were warned to end 'harmful practices, such as the publication of tabloids and sensationalist news which have a detrimental effect on the maintenance of order'. (IPYS)

EGYPT

On 6 December the independent daily *Sawt Al Umma* hit the streets for the first time in almost two years. The paper, outlawed in February 1999 (*Index* 3/1999), resumed publication following an administrative court ruling in August that declared the ban unconstitutional (*Index* 6/2000). Notable by his absence from the editorial team was political commentator **Ibrahim Eissa**, whose exclusion the court made a condition of the paper's restoration. (*Cairo Times*)

UAE-based Al-Jazeera satellite television station was ordered on 13 December to pull a programme in which prominent Muslim Brotherhood member **Essam Al Eryan** was due to appear. The station was threatened with closure in October (*Index* 1/2001). (*Cairo Times*)

On 14 December prosecutors gained leave to retry **Salaheddin Mohsen**, who is accused of defaming Islam. Mohsen was originally charged last May following complaints that his book *Shivering of the Lights* 'directed insults at the Divinity and the Prophet' (*Index* 4/2000). Although found guilty, he escaped with a suspended sentence after the judge warned against making him a 'martyr for free speech'. Angered by the court's leniency, prosecutors pressed for a second hearing. On 27 January, he was found guilty of 'disseminating extremist beliefs' and sentenced to three years' hard labour. (Egyptian Organisation for Human Rights, *Cairo Times*)

Former *Al Shahab* editor **Magdi Hussein** and board member **Salah Bedewi** were released from prison on 28 December under the traditional new year amnesty for non-dangerous prisoners. The two were convicted in August 1999 of slander (*Index* 5/1999). (*Cairo Times*)

On 8 January Minister of Culture Farouq Hosni denounced three books as 'indecent' and banned them from circulation. The novels, *Before and After* by **Tufiq Abderahman**, *The Children of the Romantic Error* by **Yasser Sha'ban** and *Forbidden Dreams* by **Mahmoud Hamed** were withdrawn after Hosni received complaints from Muslim Brotherhood MPs about the books' content. (*Cairo Times*)

On 13 January the culture ministry incinerated 6,000 books of poetry by the medieval poet **Abu Nawas**. The poems are alleged to 'violate public decency' and 'threaten moral norms' by celebrating homosexuality, revelry and carousing. The seizure was condemned by authors and publishers, anxious at the growing influence of Islamic mores on literature. Novelist **Gamal al-Ghitani** said the move put all writers at risk: 'We need to protect culture from the minister of culture,' he declared. (BBC, *Cairo Times*)

The country's gay community reported in mid-February that it has been subjected to increased harassment over the past month. A number of websites for homosexuals have been shut down, while the authorities have also forcibly closed the public bathhouses frequented by gays. (*Daily Telegraph*)

ETHIOPIA

On 12 and 13 December the editor-in-chief of *Ethiop* newspaper, **Schimellis Asfaw**, and **Kifle Mulat**, president of the Ethiopian Free Press Journalists' Association (EFJA), were ordered to report to the Central Investigation Department. Mulat has been hosting **Jon Lunn**, researcher with Article 19's Africa Programme, and preparing for EFJA's Third Congress, planned for on the 24 December. (EFJA)

Israel Sboka, publisher and editor-in-chief of the weekly *Seife Nebelhal*, and **Samson Seyoum**, former editor-in-chief of *Goh* and now working on the *Ethiop*, fled the country in mid-December. Sboka had been charged with six violations of the press law, while Kebede was accused of disseminating fabricated information. (EFJA)

Meles Shine, the editor-in-chief of *Ethiop* who was imprisoned in November 2000, was released on 7 January after posting bail of US\$1,200. His case has been adjourned until October. (EFJA)

Editor-in-chief of the *Tomar* newspaper, **Befekadu Moreda**, was arrested in Addis Ababa on 13 February and remains in custody. (EFJA)

FIJI

Filming of a special edition of the current affairs TV programme *Close-Up* was halted after police threatened to arrest its makers, it was reported on 22 February. Fiji TV CEO **Kenneth Clark** said that the programme was halted because an interviewee who took part did not reflect a 'wide enough cross-section' of the population, and that the station would have to apply for a permit to film again. Police described the planned gathering of panellists as a 'political gathering' which would be illegal without a permit. The station was attacked by supporters of coup leader George Speight last May over the filming of another *Close-Up* programme (*Index* 4/2000). (Pacific Media Watch)

FRANCE

After a legal ruling banning the sale of Nazi memorabilia on the websites of Internet firm Yahoo! (*Index* 1/2001), the California-based company announced a ban on all such sales, including groups such as the Ku Klux Klan. Yahoo! said on 2 January that it did not want to profit from items that glorified or promoted hatred. (*Daily Telegraph, Guardian*)

GABON

In January President Omar Bongo, his wife and his sister-in-law, Gisèle Opra, lodged two defamation charges against the satirical weekly *La Griffe* after the paper alleged that Opra was involved in an organ trafficking case. *La Griffe* also reported on the annexation of a piece of land without a permit by a school complex owned by the president's wife. The president's complaints were also due to the paper's mockery of his recently published memoirs, entitled *White Like Black*. On 15 February the National Communication Council suspended *La Griffe* and its supplement *Le Gri-Gri,* and temporarily prohibited editor **Michel Ongoundou** and editor-in-chief **Raphaël Ntoutoume** from practising journalism. The body justified its decision by claiming the journalists' writing bordered on 'provocation against the president' (*Index* 6/1998, 3/1999). (RSF)

GAMBIA

On 7 January **Peter Gomez**, editor-in-chief at Radio Gambia, was dismissed, apparently because of his refusal to publish a clarification by Fatou Jahumap-Cessay, the president's press director, in response to a report about President Jammeh's willingness to institute *sharia* law. A marketing assistant was also dismissed from the state-owned station. In December **Momodou Moussa Secka**, a journalist for the *Daily News*, was also dismissed because the publicly owned paper 'no longer required his services'. (RSF)

GEORGIA

Three journalists from the independent TV channel Rustavi 2 were kidnapped while covering the fate of Chechen refugees in the Pankisi area. Local ethnic Chechens mediated their release. (EIM)

GERMANY

The main opposition party, the Christian Democratic Union (CDU), called on 4 January for the resignation of Foreign Minister **Joschka Fischer** after Bettina Röhl, daughter of left-wing terrorist Ulrike Meinhof, produced photographs of the young Fischer assaulting a police officer during a 1973 demonstration in Bornheim. CDU spokesman Wolfgang Bosbach said that 'anyone who behaved like that cannot be a representative of a violence-free civil society'. Fischer refused to leave office, though he conceded that it had been an error to get involved in violent activity. Röhl is due to publish her book on the 1970s radical left, *Sag Mir Wo Du Stehst* (Tell Me Where You Stand), in April. Röhl claims that Fischer was 'obsessed with violence, wanting to take nothing from this violence other than to gain political power'. (*The Times*, *Observer*)

GHANA

The newly installed New Patriotic Party government has dropped the criminal libel case brought against **Eben Quarcoo**, former editor of the *Free Press*, and **Kofi Koomson**, publisher of the *Ghanaian Chronicle* (*Index* 1/2001). On 19 February the new attorney general led a team of lawyers to the court to prevent the presiding judge from reading his judgment in the case, in which the papers had carried a story that the Jerry Rawlings administration had engaged in drug smuggling. (West African Journalists Association)

GREECE

Television journalist **Makis Triantafyllopoulos** (*Index* 6/1998) was arrested on 20 December while leaving a prosecutor's office where he had been giving evidence over alleged police corruption. The arrest concerned old social security debts, but it was contended that the arrest was abusive and amounted to intimidation. (Greek Helsinki Monitor and Minority Rights Group)

The prefect of Lesbos, Dimitris Vounatsos, accused journalists of 'terrorist journalistic pimping' for publishing a document containing instructions to prefecture personnel on how to treat guests. In a letter published in the local newspaper *Democratis* on 28 December, Vounatsos claimed that the document had been stolen and that the journalists were guilty of publishing stolen material. (Greek Helsinki Monitor and Minority Rights Group)

GUINEA

On 14 February the editor of the weekly *Nouvel Observateur*, **Aboubacar Sakho**, was sentenced in Conakry to ten months' imprisonment and ordered to pay a fine of one million Guinean francs. On 15 January the newspaper had published an article criticising Justice Minister Abou Camara's decision to relieve certain magistrates of their duties. The author stated that this was the responsibility and power of the president only. In response, the justice minister lodged a complaint. Aboubacar Sakho was taken to Conakry prison, where the authorities refused journalists permission to visit. This is the first time in four years that a journalist has been sentenced to imprisonment in Guinea. (RSF)

HAITI

On 23 December Caraibes FM suspended its news programmes in response to telephone threats from sources close to the ruling Lavalas Party (*Index* 1/2001). On 27 December Rotation FM's office was surrounded by armed men linked to the municipality, prompting director **Amos Duboirant** to appear the following day on a different station to protest against their action. (RSF, Agence Haitienne de Presse)

HUNGARY

On 27 November it was reported that journalist **Peter Aradi** was brutally beaten and threatened with a gun twice; once while dining at a restaurant with friends and again at the police station. After being released he was forced to say something in Serbian while kneeling with a Bible. (ANEM)

INDEX INDEX

INDIA

Concerns were raised recently that the charge of criminal contempt had become so broadly defined that it would increasingly be used to stifle calls for judicial accountability, and other forms of dissent. The issue arose after **S K Sundaram**, a lawyer based in Chennai, had his six-month jail sentence for criminal contempt of court suspended by the Supreme Court for a month on 15 December on the understanding that he promise not to engage in more 'criminal contempt'. Sundaram had asked in a telegram that Chief Justice A S Anand step down because he had passed retirement age. (*Frontline*)

Vineet Narain, editor, printer and publisher of the investigative journal *Kalchakra*, was notified on 26 December that he would have to explain why contempt proceedings should not be taken against him for alleging that Chief Justice A S Anand had abused his authority to materially benefit his family in two land deals. (*Frontline*)

Surinder Singh Oberoi, a journalist with Agence France-Presse and a correspondent with RSF (*Index* 5/1997), was assaulted and threatened with death in Srinagar on 19 January by G M Dar, an officer with the police special forces. (RSF)

Recent Publications: *India: Words into Action: recommendations for the prevention of torture* (AI, January 2001, pp 64); *India: Appeal Cases* (AI,

January 2001, pp 16); *The Law of Domestic Violence: A users' manual for women* (Women's Legal Aid Centre, Delhi, February 2001).

INDONESIA

Oswald Iten, a Swiss journalist for *Neve Zurchen Zeitung*, was arrested on 2 December in Jayapura and detained for 12 days for taking pictures. He was suspected of breaking immigration law that prevents foreign journalists from reporting without a press visa. (RSF)

IRAN

On 9 December a court in Tabriz, capital of the province of East Azerbaijan, banned the daily *Ahrar* for three months and fined its editor, **Mohammed-Hossein Kouze-Gar**, 55 million rials (US$31,427) for 'spreading false news'. (RSF)

Naser Zarafshan, a lawyer for the pro-reform writers **Mohammad Jafar Pouyandeh** and **Mohammad Mokhtari** assassinated in December 1998 (*Index* 1/1999, 2/1999), was arrested in Shiraz after speaking out against the killings, it was reported on 11 December. (Associated Press)

On 12 December it was reported that detained writer, lawyer and editor **Mehrangiz Kar** had been diagnosed with breast cancer and was being denied permission to seek medical help overseas. Since her detention in April 2000 for participating in an academic conference in Berlin, Kar –

former editor of the now banned *Zan* literary review – is believed to be facing three new charges: for violating the observance of *hejab*; denying the Islamic necessity of *hejab*; and propagating against the Islamic Republic of Iran. On 15 January it was reported that Kar had been sentenced to four years in jail for attending the Berlin conference. (RSF)

Ezzatollah Sahabi (*Index* 5/2000), 75, former editor of the banned *Iran-e-Farda*, was arrested on 17 December. He was charged with 'insulting the Guide (of the Islamic Republic) Ayatollah Ali Khamenei, and 'propaganda against the regime' for comments made at Amir-Kabir University, Tehran, on 26 November. It was reported on 15 January that Sahabi was also being sentenced to four and a half years in jail for his participation in the Berlin conference, 'Iran after the elections', held in April 2000. (RSF)

It was reported on 15 January that other participants in the Berlin conference have also been prosecuted. **Khalil Rostamkhani** (*Index* 5/2000, 1/2001), a translator at the German embassy and a journalist with the *Daily News* and *Iran Echo*, was jailed for nine years for organising the conference, though he did not attend. During the trial the prosecution had demanded the death penalty. A fellow translator at the German embassy, **Saeed Sadr**, is to serve up to nine years in a Birjand jail for helping to organise the conference. **Akbar Ganji** (*Index* 4/2000, 1/2001), a journalist with *Sobh-e-Emrouz*, was sentenced to ten years in jail and five years' internal exile – namely being forbidden to leave the country or to live in Tehran – at the end of the sentence. Ganji – who had investigated the killings of dissidents in late 1998 (*Index* 1/1999) – claimed at his trial that he had been tortured. Publisher **Shahla Lahiji** was given four years' imprisonment for acting against national security and disseminating propaganda against the Islamic regime. **Fariborz Raisdana**, a prominent economist, received a three-year jail term, to be served as a five-year suspended sentence. **Shahla Sherkat** and **Khadejeh Haji-Moghadam** were both fined. (RSF, WiPC, Gulf 2000)

Massoud Behnoud (*Index* 6/2000), a journalist for the *Adineh* daily, was released on bail on 16 December after being arrested in August. (RSF)

Eighteen people stood before the Tehran military court on 23 December accused of involvement in the late 1998 killings of leading reformists and intellectuals. On 27 January three of the defendants were sentenced to death and two to life imprisonment. There was widespread dissatisfaction with the trial, which was held in secret and left key questions unanswered. A lawyer for two of the defendants said that, during the trial, he had tried to introduce ten witnesses to testify that the killings were ordered by the then minister of intelligence, Ghorbanali Dorinajafabadi,

but the court refused to hear them. Dorinajafabadi currently occupies a senior government position in the judiciary. (HRW, RSF)

It was reported on 2 January that **Ali Afsahi**, editor-in-chief of the cultural and sports publication *Cinama-Varzech*, has been sentenced to four months' imprisonment. Afsahi, a clergyman as well as a journalist, was convicted for 'insulting and libelling the clergy' at a speech he gave in Bouchehr about Iranian cinema. (RSF)

On 10 January **Ibrahim Nabavi** (*Index* 5/2000, 6/2000, 1/2001) was sentenced by the press court to eight months' imprisonment. Nabavi, a contributor to now banned reformist papers such as *Jameh* and *Tous*, was sentenced for 'deceptive publications, insults against officials of the regime and unfounded accusations'. (RSF)

Kiyan, a ten-year-old independent journal specialising in philosophy, religion and literature, has been closed by the authorities, it was reported on 17 January. The summary ban was ordered by Saeed Motazavi, a judge in Branch 1410 of the Tehran General Court, which deals with alleged press offences. Mortazavi stated that *Kiyan* had published lies, disturbed public opinion and insulted sacred religion. (HRW)

Naghi Afchari, editor of the weekly *Hadis*, was arrested and detained on 27 January. He was charged with 'criticising the judiciary' and having

published a cartoon which was 'insulting' to the Iranian courts. *Hadis* was banned the same day. (RSF)

Hoda Saber, one of the editors of the banned monthly *Iran-e-Farda*, was imprisoned on 28 January. His wife has not been told where Saber is being detained since his arrest on 17 December. (RSF)

Journalists **Genevieve Abdo** and **Jonathan Lyons** had to leave Tehran on the night of 2–3 February. Abdo, of the *Guardian*, and her husband Lyons, Tehran bureau chief for Reuters, say they were forced to leave after being told they would face prosecution for interviewing political prisoner **Akbar Ganji**. On 23 January the *International Herald Tribune* published an interview with Ganji, who spoke of a 'possible backlash of the conservative establishment'. The general director of the foreign press, Mohammed-Reza Kochvaght, announced that the two journalists had 'acted in contradiction with rules and ethics and distorted Akbar Ganji's statements'. On 4 February, the Ministry of Culture announced that Lyons was barred from returing to Tehran. (RSF)

IRELAND

A Dublin court heard on 6 December that the assassination of journalist **Veronica Guerin** (*Index* 5/1996, 1/1997) was devised by drugs baron John Gilligan in order to avoid prosecution for an alleged assault and to protect his drugs empire. Prosecutor Peter Charleton said that

Gilligan's gang used vicious and violent threats against anyone who threatened his will. (*Guardian*)

KENYA

On 10 December police attacked **Collin Kwayu**, a photojournalist with *People Daily*, moments before a meeting by the lobby group Muungano wa Mugeuzi was due to start in Naivasha. Kwayu had attempted to take pictures of police in riot gear who were patrolling the streets to ensure the rally did not take place. The paper finally secured the journalist's release. (NDIMA)

The Communications Commission of Kenya ordered the immediate closure of the newly launched Kenya Internet Exchange Point, it was reported on 12 December. The exchange was only the second to be established south of the Sahara. Local ISPs said they would now be 'forced to route all local traffic through international links before the same comes back to Kenya'. (NDIMA)

Argwing Odera, a well-known investigative freelance journalist, went missing for several days from 1 January while covering a protest against a Japanese-funded power project in Sondu, Western Province. The journalist had been accused of trespassing and 'uttering words which indicated, or implied, that the community can destroy the buildings'. According to his lawyer, he sustained a bullet wound to the shoulder. Odera was released

on a bond for KSh100,000 (approximately US$1,290). (NDIMA, Digital Freedom Network)

The Nairobi High Court has ordered the hearing of a case against **Njehu Gatabaki**, publisher and editor-in-chief of *Finance* magazine, for publishing an allegedly libellous article against President Daniel arap Moi on 8 December. The article was entitled 'Moi ordered Molo massacre'. (NDIMA)

The Nation Media Group faces a a Ksh100m (approx. US$1.3m) defamation suit from Julius Sunkuli, a cabinet minister, because the company linked his name with the murder of US Catholic priest **Father John Kaiser** in Naivasha on 24 August (*Index* 6/2000). The *Daily Nation* said that Kaiser was pursuing cases of 'defilement' by a senior cabinet minister when he was shot dead. It further added that 60 women had put their names on a petition against a senior minister who, they claimed, had 'run amok' in the district. (NDIMA)

Police attacked journalists in the western town of Kisumu, it was reported on 12 February. *East African Standard*'s Kisumu bureau chief **Haroun Wandalo**, Kenyan Television Network (KTN) cameraman **Avid Ohito** and photographer **Jacob Otieno** were injured. ((NDIMA)

KYRGYSTAN

On 1 February the Sverdlov district court of Bishkek began considering a lawsuit by

Omurbek Tekebaev, vice-speaker of a parliamentary chamber, against pro-government journalist **Kalen Sydykova**. Tekebaev accuses her of publishing incorrect information in the newspaper *Argument* on 27 October, two days before the presidential poll in which he stood as an opposition candidate. (RFE/RL)

On 14 February MP Akbokon Tashtanbekov filed a lawsuit against the daily *Vecherny* and its journalist, **Larisa Li**, over an article, 'Division of property by fists', published on 8 September, that he claims is inaccurate. He is demanding compensation of 150,000 soms (US$3,000) from the paper and 50,000 soms (US$1,000) from the journalist. (RFE/RL)

On 22 February **Mamat Sabyrov**, editor-in-chief of the independent weekly *Asaba*, said the paper was under threat of closure due to being valued at only 300,000 soms (US$22,000) by officials at the Leon Technics Company. Days before, the court of arbitration ruled that the paper must pay 1m soms (US$22,000) to the Canadian Kumtor Operating Company (KOC). According to Sabyrov, any money transferred to the paper's bank accounts could be immediately seized by KOC. (RFE/RL)\

The independent weekly *Res Publica* is under threat of closure after its printing house, Uchkun, received a letter from the Pervanai district court of Bishkek ordering it not to print. Editor-in-chief **Zamira Sydykora** told journalists that the court is demanding immediate payment of two fines. Two years ago, the court sentenced *Res Publika* to pay 50,000 soms (US$1,000) to Amanbek Karypkulov, president of the national TV and radio corporation, after publishing a critical letter from its employees. A further 20,000 soms ($US400) is owed to Sardarkek Botaliev, who sued the paper after it had written about him organising a duplicate committee under the same name as the Kyrgyz Committee for Human Rights (*Index* 1/0001). (RFE/RL, CJES)

MACEDONIA

On 28 November shots were fired into the front door of the home of journalist **Aleksandr Comovski**, and again on 27 December. Later that day, the transmitters of the national broadcasters TV A1 and TV Sitel were deprived of electricity. In addition, unknown persons called TV Sitel and informed employees that a bomb had been planted on their premises. (Macedonian Press Centre)

MALAWI

On 12 December a journalist at *Weekend Nation*, **Denis Mzembe**, was called in for questioning by fiscal police over an article in which he alleged that a company belonging to the wife of President Bakili Muluzi was involved in a corrupt cement deal. Mzembe was detained, but refused to disclose his sources. (MISA)

MALAYSIA

Journalists from online newspaper malaysiakini.com were banned from attending and reporting on any government activities in February on the grounds that it is not a licensed publication. The home minister was quoted as saying the reason was the website's critical approach to the government. On 4 March, the home minister withdrew the ban. (IPI, BBC News, Free media Movement)

MAURITANIA

On 14 December Interior Minister Dah Ould Abdeljellil ordered the seizure of the Arabic-language weekly *Al Alam* after the publication of articles about the arrests of three officers on 28 November, and a separate campaign against the arrest of opposition political figures. Two days later the publication was banned. (RSF)

MOROCCO

The French weekly *Courrier International* and the Spanish magazine *Epoca* were seized in mid-December while awaiting distribution. The *Courrier International* contained a special report that included pieces by the editors of banned papers *Le Journal*, *Assahifa* and *Demain* (*Index* 1/2001), while *Epoca* featured an article entitled 'Morocco: the totalitarian temptation'. (RSF)

On 12 January the ministry of justice lifted the ban imposed in early December on *Assahif* and *Le Journal* newspapers, three days after **Aboubakr**

Jammai, the latter's editor, began a hunger strike. Though the authorities reissued licences to the two papers, *Demain* remains proscribed. (BBC, RSF)

Al Ittihad Al Ichtiraki photographer **Hannouda Taibi** was detained in Casablanca on 23 January after taking pictures of police headquarters. When officers spotted Taibi, they took him inside the station where he was beaten and placed in solitary confinement. Taibi was released the next day, but his camera and personal belongings were confiscated. (RSF)

MOZAMBIQUE

Salamao Moyana, editor of the independent weekly *Savana*, received threatening telephone calls on 14 December. Moyana and the paper's senior reporter, **Paulo Machava**, were told they were on a death list because, the anonymous caller said, 'you talk too much' and 'stick your noses into things'. (MISA)

NAMIBIA

On 10 January Mocks Shivute, permanent secretary in the ministry of foreign affairs, information and broadcasting, demanded that the directors of the government-funded *New Era* newspaper take Zambian-born journalist **David Kashweka** to task for his 'exaggerated and distorted' claims. On 9 January Kashweka published an article in the *Namibian* entitled 'Paying the price for the enduring Angolan conflict'. On 26 January Minister of

Foreign Affairs, Information and Broadcasting Theo-Ben Gurirab appointed new boards of directors at the Namibian Press Agency (NAMPA) and New Era Publications Corporation. Among the five-member board of NAMPA is Mocks Shivute. (MISA)

It was reported on 2 February that Judge President Pio Teek had laid charges of contempt against the dailies *Namibian* and *Die Republikein*, as well as the Society of Advocates, for their comments and alleged interference in a case against José Domingos Sikunda, UNITA's former Namibian representative. The dailies accused him of delaying the implementation of a court order against Sikunda. (MISA)

NEPAL

On 27 December it was reported that cinemas across the country had stopped screening Indian films after an alleged anti-Nepal slur by Bollywood star **Hrithik Roshan**. The remarks were allegedly made during a television interview. The ban will remain in place until Roshan apologises. (BBC News)

On 16 January Minister of Information and Communications Jay Prakash Prasad Gupta notified the country's 11 private radio stations that they were banned from broadcasting their own news. Gupta said they would have to send their reports for ministry approval a minimum of one week prior to broadcast. (RSF, BBC News)

NIGERIA

On 7 January unknown assailants attacked **Mallam Mohammed Ahmad Kwallam** in Kano, correspondent of Voice of America, leaving him critically wounded. Nothing was taken from the journalist by his attackers. (IFJ)

The offices of Media Techniques Limited in Lagos, publishers of *City People*, was attacked in the early hours of 10 January by armed persons and occupants were held hostage for two hours. A security man with *City People*, **Kamsulum Kazeem**, was shot dead and another occupant received machete wounds. (Nigeria Media Monitor)

PAKISTAN

On 10 January it was reported that Karachi police fired tear gas and baton-charged a crowd protesting against the use of blasphemy law to victimise religious minorities (*Index* 4/2000). The demonstration was organised by the All Faiths Spiritual Movement International, a body that represents Christians and some minority Muslim sects. (BBC News)

The daily *Frontier Post* was closed by the Peshawar police on 29 January and five employees arrested under the blasphemy law, following publication of a letter in that day's opinion page entitled 'Why Muslims hate Jews'. The detained employees were **Aftab Ahmed**, news editor, **Imtiaz Hussain**, chief reporter, **Qazi Ghulam**

Sarwar, the senior sub-editor, **Munawar Mohsin**, opinion-page editor and **Wajihul Hassan**, layout designer. **Shahid Afridi**, who is not an employee but was on the premises at the time of the raid, was arrested on charges of disrupting public order. The police are also searching for managing editor **Mehmood Afridi** and co-editor **Javed Nazir**. On 30 January the *Frontier Post* placed prominent apologies on the front pages of all Urdu and English-language dailies, blaming it on disgruntled employees. Nonetheless, a mob of protesters burned down the *Frontier Post*'s printing press, causing severe damage. On 31 January police arrested six people from *Maidan*, the paper's Urdu sister paper, and interrogated them for several hours about the whereabouts of Mehmood Afridi before they were released. The same day cadres of the Islamic party *Jammat-e-Islami* beat photographers **Haider Shah**, from *News International* daily, and **Shahzad**, from the Urdu-language daily *Al-Akhbar,* when they tried to take pictures of crowds rioting. On 1 February police raided the Peshawar offices of the Urdu-language *Jasarat*, a paper linked to the *Jammat-e-Islami*, on the grounds that its publication of extracts from the letter was an attempt to fuel the demonstrations against the *Frontier Post*. On 15 February, Imtiaz Hussain, Qazi Ghulam Sarwar and Wajihul Hassan were released from police custody. (CPJ, RSF, *Guardian*, Pakistan Press Foundation)

PALESTINE

Three masked men walked into the Beach Hotel in Gaza City on January 17 and shot dead **Hisham Mekki**, 54, chief of Palestinian radio-television. Mekki was a member of Yasser Arafat's Fatah movement and known for an opulent lifestyle. He is the most prominent of the 360 Palestinians to have been killed since September 2000. The Palestinian Authority blamed collaborators for the killing, but others point the finger at Israel, which denied responsibility. (RSF, *International Herald Tribune, Daily Telegraph*, BBC)

PANAMA

A bill to abolish the 'insult laws', which empower state representatives to imprison journalists for 'lack of respect', was defeated on 12 December, undermining President Mireya Moscoso's 20 December 1999 repeal of the 'gag laws' used by the interior ministry to close down newspapers and censor the media. Since then, the authorities have relied on the more vaguely defined 'insult laws' to quieten critics. Just days after the 14 July trial of reporter **Jean Marcel-Chéry** (*Index* 5/2000), **Carlos Singares**, editor of the daily *El Siglo*, was sentenced to 20 months' imprisonment for an article published early that year. Chéry's paper, *El Panama América,* received a phone call from President Moscoso herself, threatening the paper with a libel suit if it published a memorandum questioning the provenance of a helicopter she was using. (RSF)

PARAGUAY

Salvador Medina, reporter and chairman of the board of directors of Capibary community radio station Ñemity, was shot dead on 5 January. The reporter had received death threats after exposing alleged local mafia activity. (IAPA, Sindicato de Periodistas del Paraguay, RSF)

On 19 December **Mauri Konig**, reporter for Brazilian daily *O Estado do Paraná*, was beaten up by three men armed with sticks and chains. One assailant was wearing police uniform. Konig had been investigating reports that young Brazilian men were serving in the Paraguayan army and National Police Force. (IAPA)

PERU

Ángela Talledo, photojournalist with daily *Liberación*, was assaulted on 12 December by Delia Vergara, mayor of the Chaclacayo district of Lima, after taking photos at the entrance to Lima's Thirty-Third Criminal Court. Talledo was awaiting the arrival of the former head of the National Intelligence Service, Julio Salazar Monroe. Vergara was herself going to appear in a criminal court for calling lawyer Marco Tulio Gutierrez a 'blackmailer' and objected to Talledo taking photos of her. Later (IPYS)

Five journalists serving prison sentences of between 12 and 20 years – **Hermes Rivera Guerrero** (*Index* 1/1995, 5/1995), **Antero Gargurevich Oliva** (*Index* 7/1993, 3/1994, 4/1994. 5/1994), **Juan de Mata Jara Berrospi**, **Javier Tuanama Valera** (*Index* 1/1991, 2/1991, 3/1991, 1/1995) and **Pedro Carranza Ugaz** – are having their cases reviewed, it was announced on 18 December. All stand accused of collaborating with, or justifying the actions of, armed insurrections that took place in the past decade. In some cases they were convicted on the basis of accusations that were retracted at a later date; in other cases, confessions were extracted under torture. (IFJ)

On 21 December the offices of Arequipa daily *El Pueblo* were attacked by about 50 armed assailants led by the newspaper's former director, William Cornejo Tejada, and its former lawyer, Agripino Gutiérrez. Both are involved in a legal conflict with the current management. Cornejo and Gutiérrez were removed from their posts for mismanagement of the paper's administrative and financial affairs in 1993. It took seven hours to remove the assailants. (IFJ)

Alejandro Vílchez Pardo, host of *El Centinela del Pueblo* programme on Talara radio station Dennys, received death threats following comments made on his programme about the criminal charges filed by the Talara provincial attorney against the municipal authorities for embezzlement of funds. Owner of the radio station Faustina Zapata de Halanocca then decided to cancel Vílchez Pardo's contract. (IFJ)

Journalist **Alberto Pintado Villaverde** reported on 25 December that his family had been receiving death threats since he made reports on alleged corruption in the Provincial Municipality of Utcubamba. Pintado Villaverde, director of radio programme *Compartiendo* and reporter for Galaxia Super Stereo and Canal 2 radio stations, suggested that municipal director Polidoro Sologastúa Damián was responsible for the threats. (IFJ)

Raúl Herrera Soria, a correspondent for Panamericana Television, and **Nicolás Prokopiu**, head of a police news programme, were leaving a Popular Christian Party (PCP) press conference on 4 January when they were attacked by members of the Loreto Patriotic Front protesting against the PCP presidential candidate, Lourdes Flores Nano. (IPYS)

Journalists **Faustino Sandoval Damián**, **Hubert Flores**, **Nelson Serna La Madrid**, **Luis Ramírez** and **Leoncio Longa Morales** were attacked by a mob with stones and sticks on 15 January. The mob also attempted to set Sandoval on fire. (IFJ)

César Hernán Vásquez Ríos, editor of the magazine *Integración*, received death threats from Raúl Bernabé Mercado Solano. It was reported on 19 January that when Mercado Solano realised that Vásquez Ríos was about to file a complaint against him, he issued the threats and assaulted the journalist's sons. Vásquez Ríos had reported

that a National Peruvian Police vehicle had been lent to Mercado Solano because the person to whom it was licensed did not need it. (IFJ)

On 30 January, Victor Hugo Salvatierra, from the acting public prosecutor's office, brought criminal charges against **Nicolás Lúcar**, journalist and director of the television programme *Tiempo Nuevo*. Lúcar was charged with aggravated contempt of President Valentín Paniagua, Attorney General Nelly Calderón and President of Congress Carlos Ferrero Costa, after an alleged former security agent made certain statements against them during an interview on *Tiempo Nuevo*. (IPYS)

It was reported on 2 February that Judge Luisa Sotomayor has ordered that Argentine Héctor Faisal be prevented from leaving the country. Faisal, who is linked to Vladimir Montesinos, is accused of defaming a number of individuals opposed to the former government via the website of the Association for the Defence of the Truth (APRODEV). Faisal accused Soberón of having misappropriated funds collected by the journalist **César Hildebrandt** (*Index* 2/1998, 4/1998, 4/1999, 6/1999, 2/2000, 3/2000, 4/2000, 5/2000) from contributions deposited in bank accounts in aid of former agent **Leonor La Rosa**, who was tortured under Montesinos' orders by the National Intelligence Service. Augusto Zuñiga, lawyer for the Association for Human Rights (APRODEH), filed a

complaint against Faisal for defamation and slander, asking for US$300,000 in damages, and accused Faisal of being used by Montesinos as a means of discrediting journalists. Faisal's lawyer maintains that he was merely reproducing material that had already been published in the dailies. (IPYS)

On 28 January the host of the programme *La Voz del Pueblo*, **Rosiberto Ushiñahua Ushiñahua**, was assaulted by the director of the Requena district education department, Professor Félix Masuca Pizango. Ushiñahua was broadcasting a communiqué from the Requena Patriotic Front in which the management of the regional education department was called into question; Masuca Pizango broke into the broadcast booth and punched the journalist in the face. (IPYS)

Journalist **Iván Cubas Coronado** was released from Trujillo's El Milagro jail on 1 February after his conviction for aggravated defamation of a functionary of the La Libertad High Court was overturned. He was convicted on 23 August and had been detained since September. (IPYS)

The 2,400 'Vladi-videos', recorded by former spy-chief Vladimir Montesinos and seized from his apartment late last year, have revealed the widespread corruption of the country's powerful elite. The public appetite for these videos in the run-up to the 8 April election is insatiable; the political repercussions have angered many presidential candidates into claiming that the release of the videos has been manipulated. The Roman Catholic Church has offered to guard the tapes – which sources say feature politicians and military officials in sexually compromising situations – with the intention of returning them to the featured individuals. Montesinos, meanwhile, has reportedly been undergoing facial surgery so that he can avoid recognition. (BBC, CNN, *International Herald Tribune*)

PHILIPPINES

On 12 December a church-run transmitter site (DXMS) in Catabato City was bombed, leaving one man injured. The bombing was allegedly aimed at preventing the radio from airing an interview with **Zamsamin Ampatua** in which he criticises the Moro Islamist Liberation Front (MILF). Eid Kabalu, MILF's spokesperson denies any involvement. (Centre for Media Freedom and Responsibility)

On 3 January, **Rolando Ureta**, director of the Radio Mindanao Network (RMN), was shot dead in Aklan. Due to his outspoken comments on local government involvement with drug lords, he had received death threats since August. Rolando Ureta follows **Olimpio Jalapit**, another RMN broadcaster who was shot dead on 17 November 2000 in Pagadian (*Index* 1/2001). (Centre for Media Freedom and Responsibility)

PORTUGAL

Journalist **Lopes Gomes da Silva** brought a successful case to the European Court of Human Rights after the Lisbon Court of Appeal held that da Silva's editorial in magazine *Público*, criticising the People's Party's electoral candidate Silva Resende in 1993, was libellous. The judgment on 29 November 1995, stated that expressions such as 'grotesque', 'rustic' and 'coarse' were insulting and personal. The European Court found that da Silva's editorial was not without factual basis and that 'journalists were allowed to resort to a degree of prevarication'. (Council of Europe Information Note No. 22)

ROMANIA

A few days after the December electoral defeat of anti-Semitic presidential candidate Vladim Tudor, thugs broke into the Jewish Museum in Bucharest, shouting: 'Where is the soap made of human fat?' (Greek Helsinki Monitor)

RUSSIA

Oleg Luriye, Moscow reporter with *Novaya Gazeta*, was surrounded and then attacked by four men on 16 December, leaving him with concussion and facial wounds from a straight razor. The night before the attack, Luriye accused the Kremlin of singling out President Vladimir Putin's opponents for criminal persecution and ignoring allegations of corruption about Kremlin insiders. The attack is thought to be linked to a recent Luriye article which accused Alexander Voloshin, Putin's chief of staff, of illegally enriching himself through deals involving media owner Boris Berezovsky. Three days before the attack, policeman seized files on Voloshin and Berezovsky from *Novaya Gazeta*'s office. (CJES)

It was reported on 23 January that reporting on the massive breakdown of power and heat in the Soviet Far East and the continuing war in Chechnya has all but disappeared, following the government's new control of Media-MOST's NTV, once the only independent television network (*Index* 4/2000, 5/2000, 1/2001). Ted Turner of CNN and George Soros's attempt to secure the company's future independence by buying 25% of NTV's shares was halted after a Kremlin meeting on 15 January. The following day police raided NTV's offices and a top Media–MOST executive was arrested. Computers at the subsidiary Image Bank remain frozen as a result of the 30 raids carried out on Media-MOST, threatening to pull NTV, its regional network TNT and radio station Ekho Moskvy off the air. In addition, on 15 December, tax authorities announced plans to liquidate NTV, NTV Plus, the Sem Dnei publishing house, *Segodnya* newspaper and the Media-MOST holding company, claiming that their net assets are less than required under article 99 of Civil code. (*International Herald Tribune*, RFE/RL)

Edmond Pope, a US businessman sentenced to 20 years

• •

ELENA BONNER
Truth lying in state

We live in a state of lies. The great lie calls Russia a democratic state. Barely had election procedures been introduced in the country than they were violated. Then came the appointment of Putin as Yeltsin's heir – as if Russia were a monarchy. Electoral machinations have spread to elections for governors, which are decided largely by money and not the voters. And where there are no valid elections, then there is no democracy. When it comes to Belarus, everyone agrees on this. But they are afraid to say it about Russia.

A chilling development of recent years has been a series of arrests and court trials that smack of lawlessness. These include the cases of US businessman Edmond Pope, diplomat Valentin Moiseyev, journalist Grigory Pasko and navy captain Sergei Nikitin, all of whom were accused of spying. And we should not forget journalist Andrei Babitsky, who last year faced shamelessly trumped-up charges for reporting the truth from Chechnya. And yet not a single political murder of recent years has been resolved.

The state is destroying companies and trusts that manage publications and TV stations, and creating, under its own control, others more powerful and corrupt. And while the world knows about the government's campaign against Boris Berezovsky and Vladimir Gusinsky, whose persecution is clearly coloured by anti-Semitism, very few people know about what is happening to the mass media in outlying regions. Similar affairs there end in violence too often for this is to be considered exceptional. It looks as if, in a short time, there will be no truly free and independent TV station. Instead we will have the recently promulgated 'Doctrine on Information Security', which calls for government supervision of the press and television.

It is intolerable how many lies and falsehoods have been poured into people's minds: the nuclear reactor explosion at Chernobyl, the earthquake at Neftyugansk, the loss of the Kursk submarine. At the same time we continually hear official lies in daily life, perpetuating the lies of the USSR. Just recently, a young man said to me about the Prague Spring: 'That was when the Czechs attacked us.' Truth cannot stand up to so many lies. ❑

Excerpted from a speech delivered by **Elena Bonner**, *widow of Soviet dissident Andrei Sakharov, to the Heinrich Böll Foundation and the Hannah Arendt Association in February*

• •

in prison for spying and allegedly obtaining classified blueprints for a high-speed torpedo, was pardoned by President Putin and finally left Russia on 14 December. (*Daily Telegraph*)

Journalist **Andrei Babitsky** (*Index* 4/2000, 5/2000) was ordered to pay 8,350 rubles (US$300) on 13 December for 'possessing a false passport'. Babitsky was arrested in January 2000 by Federal Forces outside Grozny after which he was handed over to Chechen rebels who provided him with an Azeri passport so they could take him to Azerbaijan. (RSF)

The fraud case against Media-MOST head **Vladmir Gusinsky** (*Index* 4/2000, 5/2000, 1/2001) was dismissed on 26 December by a Moscow court, but the prosecutor's office said it would appeal. (RFE/RL)

The espionage trial of **Igor Setyagin** of the Institute for USA and Canada reopened in Kalga Oblast on 9 January after Setyagin requested an additional lawyer and more time at proceedings held in late December. He has been held in prison for over a year accused of passing classified information about Russian nuclear submarines to the US and Britain. He claims he did not have access to classified information and based his analyses on information available from open sources. (RFE/RL)

SENEGAL

On 12 December editor **Mamadou Thierno Talla**

and journalist **Sidy Diop**, both with the Dakar daily *Le Populaire*, were summoned to the Criminal Investigation Division and interrogated for three hours about an article on ethnic rivalries in the Casamance, where there is a secessionist conflict. Their overview had included a list of the demands made by the rebel Movement of Democratic Forces. The incident follows a series of government warnings to the press about covering the separatist movement. (RSF)

SERBIA-MONTENEGRO

From May to November 2000 the OSCE journalist protection programme recorded 32 cases of violations of journalists' rights in Kosovo. They included anonymous and personal threats, assaults, one bombing, a disappearance and suspected murder, and one confirmed murder. One of the favourite targets was *Bota Sot*, one of the few to regularly report attacks against journalists. (Greek Helsinki Monitor)

On 29 November former prime minister Mirko Marjanovic laid charges against the Belgrade daily *Vecernje novosti* for disseminating false information. The paper alleged that he had a credit arrangement with the Progress Party for the purchase of apartments. (ANEM)

On 7 December satirist **Boban Miletic** had 25 of the 30 copies of his book *Cry Mother Serbia* returned to him by the police who confiscated them last June for insulting former president Slobodan Milosevic (*Index* 4/2000). 'I

will relinquish the remaining six books to the police for the sake of their education,' said Miletic.

On 13 December President Vojislav Kostunica said that the authorities are to propose new legislation aimed at clarifying the rights of the country's ethnic minorities, including provisions for regional and local autonomy and voting rights. (RFL/RL)

It was reported on 13 December that Marko Milosevic, son of the former president, has brought charges against the owners of three Belgrade dailies, *Blic*, *Vecernje Novosti* and *Glas Javnosti*, accusing them of causing damage to his honour and reputation. He asked for US$1m in compensation from each. (ANEM)

On 16 December the organisers of a blockade on the Nis-Skopje road, near Bujanovac, refused to allow journalists from the dailies *Glas javnosti* and *Danas*, and the weekly *Vranjske novine* to enter the region. They also physically attacked **Radoman Iric** of Radio B92. They accused the journalists of biased and inaccurate reporting. (ANEM)

On 30 December the Public Information Act (1998) was declared unconstitutional under Yugoslav law, though it has not been wholly removed from the statute books. The annulled clauses relate to the system of public media registration, publishing restrictions and the hefty fines which could be imposed on media during Milosevic's era. Some

67 media bodies were fined a total of US$1.2m during the lifespan of the act. (ANEM)

Emir Kusturica's film *Underground* was aired twice over the new year by RTS, but with a cut of ten minutes. It is not yet known whether the film producer and distributor Komuna Company or RTS was responsible for the cut, which included one of the most popular scenes. (ANEM)

On 10 January Montenegrin sports commentator **Branko Vujisic** was arrested at Belgrade airport on grounds that he had not responded to the military calls during the NATO air raids in 1999. He claimed he had not received a single notice, but was told that a military court had sentenced him *in absentia* to a two-year jail sentence. (ANEM)

On 20 January the managing board of the official news agency Tanjug appointed Dusan Dakovic as editor-in-chief, in spite of a recent decision that the post should be filled through open competition. Dakovic was formerly a member of the Milosevic government's extensive censorship regime. (ANEM)

On 20 January the Belgrade home of journalist **Rajko Djurdjevic** was sprayed with bullets a day after he appeared on TV Palma to discuss the situation in southern Serbia. The Belgrade daily *Glas Javnosti* reported that the doors and windows were spray-painted with anti-KLA graffiti. (ANEM)

On 24 January a federal policeman hit journalist **Andrija Igic** as he entered the foreign ministry building at the same time as members of the Association of Families of Abducted and Missing Kosovo Serbs who were due to meet The Hague Tribunal's chief prosecutor, Carla del Ponte. One guard pushed Igic and then hit him, saying that Igic had not put out a cigarette before entering a non-smoking area. At the same time, an RTS crew was attacked outside the building by demonstrators loyal to the Patriotic Alliance and the Radical Left Party. Guards failed to stop the attack and even attempted to arrest an RTS cameraman. (ANEM)

The families of the 16 employees killed in the NATO bombing of the RTS newsroom on 23 April 2000 are holding both the management and NATO responsible (*Index* 1/2001). President Kostunica has undertaken to expedite legal procedures to deal with the case. The district attorney's office has suggested that the interior minister revoke the passport of former RTS director Draglojub Milanovic to prevent him from leaving the country. (ANEM)

SIERRA LEONE

On 5 February police detained for four hours **Pius Foray**, owner and editor of the independent *Daily Democrat*, after he ran a story stating that President Ahmed Tejan Kabbah feared for his life in the aftermath of the assassination of Congolese President Laurent Kabila. Journalists at the *Demo-crat* said that Criminal Investigation Division officers conducted a search for documents relevant to the arresting officers' investigation. In a related development, the government announced a ban on all political discourse. (CPJ)

SLOVAKIA

On 14 December the first Slovak translation of Hitler's *Mein Kampf* went on sale. The book is accompanied by a 30-page commentary which stresses the book's racist, anti-Semitic and violent nature. A total of 5,000 copies have been printed. (RFL/RL)

SRI LANKA

Subramaniam Tiruchelvam, Point Pedro correspondent for the government-owned daily *Thinakaran* and the Tamil-language *Valampuri*, was arrested on 2 January in Colombo by a Terrorist Investigation Division officer. Subsequent to his detention, Tiruchelvam's wife has only been able to visit him once, and he has reportedly been tortured. Douglas Devananda – the leader of the Eelam Peoples Democratic Party, a minister in the new coalition government, and the man assumed to have ordered journalist **Mylvaganam Nimalrajan** killed last October (*Index* 1/2001) – is alleged to have been behind Tiruchelvam's arrest. (RSF, *Lanka Academic*, Free Media Movement, BBC)

On 13 January army troops arrested nine Tamil undergraduates while they were putting up posters in the northern Jaffna peninsula calling for President Kumaratunga's government to match a unilateral month-long truce begun by the Tamil Tigers separatist group (LTTE) on 24 December. Under the country's emergency laws, putting up anti-government posters is an offence. (BBC, Agence France-Presse)

It was reported on 24 January that **Keerthi Warnakulasuriya**, defence analyst for the Sinhala-language *Irida Divaina* weekly, would be asked by the Criminal Investigation Bureau to reveal his sources for a story in which he claimed that three LTTE spies flew to Jaffna under military escort during a guided tour for the media. Concealing information regarding the LTTE is a criminal offence under the Prevention of Terrorism Act. (*Lanka Academic*)

Faiz Mustapha, chairman of the state-appointed Human Rights Commission (HRC), publicly criticised the ongoing censorship of military news on 27 January, saying that the law should not block media from raising issues of public accountability in the name of national security. The HRC did not advocate abolishing censorship (*Index* 4/1998, 1/2000, 4/2000, 6/2000), but went on to recommend that the current censorship authority be replaced with a censorship panel that includes a senior journalist, as well as a person with military experience. (*Times of India*)

Responsibility for a grenade attack against the main office of the British NGO Oxfam on

31 January was claimed by the National Front Against Tigers, a Sinhalese extremist group (*Index* 2/2000). In a veiled reference to Norway, currently trying to facilitate peace talks between the government and the LTTE, the group accused Oxfam of being funded by Scandinavian countries and using its projects to 'give cover to' the LTTE. (Asian News International, BBC, Agence France-Presse)

On 1 February Junior Health Minister Janaka Bandara Tennekoon was arrested for the murder of two supporters of the opposition United National Party during elections in Dambulla on 10 October (*Index* 1/2001). (*Times of India*)

On 13 February suspected members of the presidential security division forced their way into the home of opposition United National Party activist **H H A Kamala** and set it on fire. In a recent opposition protest, Kamala had dressed up as President Chandrika Kumaratunga with a bandage over her right eye to remind observers of the eye the president had injured during the LTTE attempt on her life in December 1999. (United News of India, Agence France-Presse)

The trial of two air force officers charged with invading the home of *Sunday Times* defence columnist **Iqbal Athas** in 1998 (*Index* 2 /1998, 5/1998), and violently abusing his family, was postponed for the sixth time on 16 February. (CPJ)

Recent Publication: *A Need to Know: The struggle for democratic, civilian oversight of the security sector in Commonwealth countries* (focus on Sri Lanka, Nigeria, South Africa, Barbados and St Lucia) by Neil Sammonds (Commonwealth Policy Studies Unit, London, December 2000, pp 46)

SUDAN

On 4 February **Amal Abbas**, editor of the daily *Al-Rai Al-Akher*, and **Ibrahim Hassan**, a reporter with the same newspaper, were sentenced to three months in prison for failing to pay a fine imposed after writing an article last August 2000 alleging corruption in Khartoum. (IPI)

SYRIA

It was reported on 26 January that a new ban on family visits has been placed on **Nizar Nayouf** (*Index* 6/1992, 8/1992, 10/1992, 10/1993, 6/1994, 6/1995, 5/1996, 3/1997, 1/1999, 4/1999, 4/2000). Nayouf, who suffers from leukaemia and the effects of torture, was last visited by his family in November. He began a hunger strike in February to protest against the ban. (WAN)

THAILAND

On 7 February 23 employees of the television station iTV were dismissed, apparently for expressing worries about the independence of the station's news coverage. iTV, the only independent station in the country, was taken over ten months ago by the Shin

Corporation, a company controlled by newly elected Prime Minister Thaksin Shinawatra. (CPJ)

TONGA

It was reported on 9 February that **Mateni Tapueluelu**, deputy editor of *Times of Tonga,* had appeared in court charged with criminal defamation, following the publication of an article about comments by Minister of Police Clive Edwards concerning a petition submitted by a group of police and prison officers who were made redundant in recent months. Tapueluelu, a former prison officer, and his father were among those who lost their jobs. **Kalafi Moala**, *Times of Tonga* editor, said: 'Tonga is one of the few countries in the world where libel is a criminal offence and is not dealt with by a civil court.' (Pacific Islands News Association)

It was reported on 15 February that an article alleging that senior members of the government and royal family are involved in corruption and drug smuggling had been officially condemned, though the authorities refuse to comment on the evidence. Government spokesman Eseta Fusitua dismissed as 'unethical' and 'low-level journalism' the report by **Michael Field** of the New Zealand-based *Times of Tonga,* which detailed allegations by a former policeman of 'high-level involvement in international drug running and corruption'. The source of the revelations, **Josh Liava'a**, said: 'I am not scared of them. I can destroy the Tongan govern-

ment by myself now.' (Pacific Media Watch)

TUNISIA

Three human rights campaigners, among them **Sihem Bensedrine**, director of the online magazine Kalima, were threatened and assaulted on 15 December by a group of plain-clothes police officers. The three were at the ministry of health to deliver a petition when they were confronted by security officials. Bensedrine and **Mohammed Bechri** were beaten and forced to leave, while **Omar Mestiri**, a member of the Committee for Rights in Tunisia, was bundled into a car and dumped 60km outside Tunis. (RSF)

Moncef Marzouki, founder of the National Council for Civil Liberties in Tunisia, was sentenced to 12 months' imprisonment on 30 December by a court in Tunis. Marzouki, who is banned from publishing, was charged with 'maintaining an outlawed organisation' and 'spreading false information'. (Human Rights Watch, Reuters)

Copies of the independent weekly *El Mawkif* were impounded on 12 January on the orders of Interior Minister Abdallah Kalled. The paper was seized at the printing house on the day it was due to go to press. (RSF)

The house of **Taoufik Ben Brik** (*Index* 5/1998, 2/1999, 1/2001) was surrounded by police officers on 26 January as he held a press conference to mark the launch of Kaws el Karama, an online magazine

edited by his brother **Jalel Zoghlami**. Several visitors and members of the press were prevented from entering the house; others were trailed by officers as they left; while a member of the student organisation Slah Hind was beaten. A week later, Zoghlami was struck over the head with an iron bar and pursued through the streets by a group of men brandishing daggers. None the less, the first edition of Kaws el Karama was successfully posted on the Internet with the headline, 'Ben Ali: 13 Years is Enough!' (RSF, AI)

TURKEY

The Malatya branch of the Human Rights Association (IHD) was closed on 3 December for keeping banned publications in the archive. Branch chairman **Dogan Karaoglan** said: 'The publications seized are not banned, they [have] the status of confiscated publications. They all have a definite printing house, editor-in-chief and are all legitimate.' (*Yeni Gündem*)

The printing house of the dailies *Bolu Ekspres* and *Bolu Haber* was sealed, it was reported on 5 December, reportedly for publishing an article alleging that the Bolu mayor had abused his authority. (Evrensel)

The case opened on 6 December against Islamic writer **Emine Senlikoglu**, in connection with her book *Whose victim am I?*, and against her husband **Recep Ozkan**, the publisher. The prosecution is demanding imprisonment under article 312. (Zaman)

• •

LEONID KUCHMA & YURI KRAVCHENKO
Whispers of a murder

KUCHMA: This one at *Pravda* [Georgy Gongadze], we need to decide what to do with him. He's simply gone too far.

LYTVYN: We need a case against him.

KUCHMA: That son-of-a-bitch. We should deport him to Georgia and fucking throw him out there . . . The Chechens need to steal him and throw him away. The things he writes, it's simply incredible, with caricatures of the president and dirty stories . . . someone must finance him.

KRAVCHENKO: I have people . . .

KUCHMA: The main thing is to make him an example for others . . . Drive the fucker out to Chechnya and ask for a ransom.

KRAVCHENKO: We'll get rid of him somehow . . . I need to know whether we'll be giving this assignment to someone.

KUCHMA: Yeah, yeah.

★

KUCHMA: On the matter of Gongadze, I've got information that he works and writes for *Moroz*. He started writing these articles in the summer, and we've discovered that Brodsky finances him.

KRAVCHENKO: I wouldn't be surprised if they both have connections with the socialists.

KUCHMA: They're friends all right. I remember them doing this at *Kievskie Vedomosti*. Now they're playing the same game again. That bloody Jew . . .

★

KUCHMA: I would like to ask you about the form you intend to use on Gongadze.

KRAVCHENKO: I'm – we're – working on it.

KUCHMA: I'm telling you, give him to the Chechens.

KRAVCHENKO: We'll think it through. We'll do it so that . . .

KUCHMA: I'm telling you, drive him out, undress him, leave him without his pants, let him sit there. But keep it simple.

★

KRAVCHENKO: Today we found something out.

KUCHMA: Are they looking after him?

KRAVCHENKO: Yeah yeah, they're looking. They've already found two contacts. I want to *khlopnut* [murder] him, I want to kill him, straight and simple. I'll throw him a prostitute as bait – the very best there is! He won't get away. Everything has been assigned, everything is working.

KUCHMA: That bloody Gongadze. Goodbye and good riddance. ❏

*Excerpted from the 'Gongadzegate Tapes'. In early December, Socialist Party leader Oleksandr Moroz released a secret recording of conversations between Ukrainian president Leonid Kuchma and interior minister Yuri Kravchenko, in which they are heard plotting the assassination of Internet journalist **Georgy Gongadze**, whose headless corpse was discovered late last year (*Index 1/2001*). Experts describe the tapes as '100% authentic'*

• •

On 7 December the Radio and Television Supreme Board (RTÜK) ordered the suspension of Istanbul radio station Özgür Radyo for six months for broadcasting a 'defamatory' programme which 'aims to humiliate'. The RTÜK previously ordered the station's suspension on 5 July, and again on 23 August. (RSF)

On 8 December a case opened against writer **Ahmet Altan** and **Murat Tunali**, editor-in-chief of the journal *Aktüel*, for insulting the army in an article entitled *To Be Afraid One Morning*. (*Cumhuriyet*)

It was reported on 12 December that the Diyarbakir State Security Court had opened a case against columnist **Suzan Samanci**, with the daily *Yeni Gündem,* journalists **Ayse Düzkan** and **Semra Somersan**, Kurdish activist **Sevil Eroy** and lawyer **Gülizar Tuncer** in connection with the panel entitled 'Women in Life, Women on 8 March', that was held in Diyarbakir on International Woman's Day last year. The indictment states that the defendants' speeches touched upon separatism. (*Yeni Gündem*)

Mainstream journalist and broadcaster, **Mehmet Ali Birand** (*Index* 3/1998, 4/1998, 3/2000, 6/2000), charged with broadcasting a phone interview with an inmate in Metris Prison live on CNN during a prison riot, was acquitted by Istanbul State Security Court, it was reported on 14 December. The court said that the broadcast was not a crime. (*Cumhuriyet*)

Yilmaz Akbulut and **Metin Yildirim**, distributors of the daily *Evrensel,* were detained in Istanbul on 13 December and taken to Bahçelievler Security Directorate where they were reportedly harassed and handcuffed to a radiator for seven hours. **Ayse Oyman**, reporter with *Yeni Gündem*, detained on 12 December, is still in detention. **Suat Özalp** (*Index* 6/2000), representative of the *Azadiya Welat*, and director **Seyit Karabas** who were detained on a 9 December raid of the journal's Diyarbakir offices, were remanded on 13 December. (Evrensel, *Yeni Gündem*)

Throughout 2000 the regulatory body RTÜK passed closure orders totalling 4,832 days – or nearly 13.25 years – on the nation's electronic media, according to a report on 24 December. It issued 233 warnings in the same period and opened 118 court cases, the majority of which it won. (*Yeni Binyil*)

The Istanbul State Security Court has ordered the confiscation of all copies of the book *Famous Kurdish Scientists and Intellectuals of the First Generation*, by **Mehmet Kemal Isik**, describing it as 'separatist propaganda', it was reported on 22 December. (*Yeni Gündem*)

The lawyer, playwright and human rights activist **Esber Yagmurdereli** (*Index* 2/1998, 4/1998, 6/1999, 3/2000) was freed on 18 January, after a review of his sentence under an amnesty announced in December 2000. (International PEN, Digital Freedom Network)

An unsanctioned website that lampoons the military and invites soldiers to air their complaints has caught the eye of the military's general chief of staff, according to a 7 February report in the daily *Milliyet*. Generals are looking into whether an officer is behind www.subay.net, which includes a forum called Free Fire, where soldiers can sound off on life in the army and share jokes. (Reuters, Yahoo!)

USA

The manager of a Texas shop selling adult Japanese *manga* comics is appealing against his conviction for obscenity with the support of a campaign by the Comic Book Legal Defence Fund (CBLDF). The manager was indicted on two counts of promoting obscenity, an offence which carries a possible year-long prison sentence and a US$4,000 fine. One charge was dropped after the non-profit CBLDF took on the case and defended the retailer's First Amendment rights but, in spite of inconsistencies in the verdict, the unnamed retailer was found guilty of the second. It was reported on 13 December that the CBLDF had already spent US$25,000 on this case alone. Clearly labelled 'absolutely not for children', the comic books were also racked in an '18 and over' section. (CBLDF)

Article 19 has accused the World Bank of violating international standards on freedom of information. 'The World Bank's review of its own information disclosure policy singularly fails to guarantee the public's right to know,' ran a

BUI NGOC TÂN
Tet in jail

There are no 'good' concentration camps. It is always a misfortune to be imprisoned.

'What group is he part of?'

Ban and Phuong's mother look at him in surprise, for they don't understand the prison jargon. He corrects himself.

'What work does he do at the camp?'

'Carrying excrement.'

This means that Phuong has gained the wardens' trust. Classified as a repenting prisoner and allowed to move freely in the camp by himself. The difficult part of the work: putting up with the stink. When carrying excrement baskets on one's shoulders, the load is heavy and the smell gets into your clothes and body. During the holidays, as on Tet [New Year's Day], it is worse because, when the prisoners work in the forest, they leave their waste in the forest; but when they stay in the camp, they use the toilets more, which makes the loads heavier for the excrement carriers. In addition, on the day of Tet, the prisoners are entitled to a treat of buffalo meat and bone, followed by buffalo skin. As the prisoners are hungry all year round, and as they are deprived of nutrients for long periods of time, eating meat gives them diarrhoea. The excrement becomes difficult to haul out of the toilets, since they are so full. Prisoners would line up to empty their bowels, their hands grabbing their stomachs because of the cramps. They bend over, wince. Shove one another to take their turns at the toilets. Sometimes, they defecate in their pants or underpants, and throw those in the excrement buckets. Excrement everywhere. It drops non-stop in the buckets, with the noise of gas coming out like the sound of machine guns.

There were three to take care of the excrement-carrying service; Old Goi, Chi Long Senh, an ethnic minority member, and himself, Tuan, the journalist. Old Goi said, with tears in his eyes: 'Usually at this time on New Year's Day, I would be sitting at home to receive my children, my grandchildren as well and my cousins, who would come to offer me their wishes and presents.' ❏

From A Tale of the Year 2000, *a novel by Vietnamese journalist* **Bui Ngoc Tân** *which the authorities sought to ban and destroy in March 2000. Based upon the five years Bui spent in a labour camp from 1968, extracts of the 800-page book are accessible at www.rsf.fr*

press release on 19 February, 'and allows individual countries the right to veto disclosure of information.' (A19)

The US embassy in Athens has received complaints about the failure of consulate authorities to grant a visa to the editor of a left-wing political weekly magazine who had been invited to the Columbia School of Journalists, it was reported on 30 January. **Christos Papoutsakis** has been a virulent US critic since the Colonels' dictatorship from 1967 to 1974. (Greek Helsinki Monitor)

VENEZUELA

Lawyer and university professor **Pablo Aure Sánchez** was detained by military intelligence officers on 8 January, the day after an open letter he wrote to the daily *El Nacional* was published. His detention under Article 505 of the Military Justice Code, which criminalises offending the armed forces, was brought to an end because of Sánchez's health problems. (IFJ)

On 14 and 28 January, President Hugo Chávez Frías accused the editor of daily *El Nacional*, **Miguel Enrique Otero**, of acting on 'perverse interests' when he suggested that the president was becoming more powerful. On 11 February on his weekly radio address, *Aló Presidente*, Chávez accused both national and Latin American press of participating in a conspiracy against him. (IPYS)

ZAMBIA

On 21 December editor-in-chief of the *Post* newspaper, **Fred M'membe**, was acquitted of espionage charges by Lusaka High Court (*Index* 3/1999, 5/2000, 1/2001). Judge Elizabeth Muyovwe said that the offending story in the *Post*, entitled 'Angola worries Zambia Army' had not been proven to be classified, nor that, in publishing the article, M'membe had been guilty of spying. (MISA)

On 3 January Joseph Zimba, the Lundazi district administrator and member of the ruling Movement for Multiparty Democracy (MMD), arbitrarily dismissed eight of the 15 board members of Radio Chikaya in eastern Zambia, one of only six community stations in the country. Zimba replaced the members with police and officials sympathetic to the government. Zimba argues that the mass dismissal was part of a move to 'foster transparency' and serve the Lundazi people. (MISA)

On 26 January **Chali Nondo**, a reporter for the *Monitor*, and **Stanford Hlazo**, MP for the opposition United Party for National Development (UNPD), were called separately for questioning by police in relation to an article published in the *Monitor* in the 19–25 January edition. The article warned President Chiluba against running for a third term in the light of President Kabila of Congo's recent assassination. Nondo was questioned for about an hour in the presence of his lawyer. Both he

and Hlazo and expected to be charged under Section 91 of the Penal Code, which deals with violence and breaches of the peace. (MISA)

ZIMBABWE

In the first week of December, the independent *Daily News* published a series of articles alleging a massive corruption scandal, involving senior state officials and President Robert Mugabe, in the award of a tender for the new airport. On 9 December Justice Minister Patrick Chinamasa announced that the government asked the attorney general's office to consider instituting criminal defamation proceedings against the editor and the publisher. (MISA)

On 16 December a reporter at the *Zimbabwe Independent*, **Brian Hungwe**, was manhandled and threatened at a local club by Kindness Paradza, the co-ordinator of the National Development Assembly (NDA) and former president of the Zimbabwe Union of Journalists. The incident was apparently provoked by an article that appeared in the paper in which it was claimed that that the NDA was financed by both ZANU-PF ruling party and the First Bank Corporation. (MISA)

On 10 and 11 January a photographer for the *Daily News*, **Tsvangirai Mkwazhi**, was harassed and detained. The first incident occurred in court when Mkwazhi attempted to take photographs of defendant Agnes Rusike, a war veteran who leads farm invasions in the Norton farming area. Five prison officers and a policeman rushed to seize the camera and expose the film. The following day Mkwazhi was briefly detained after taking picture of police officers removing the Zimbabwe Republic Police caravan from the centre of Harare. He was taken to the police station and interrogated for 45 minutes. Mkwazhi was released after the intervention of his editors. (MISA)

On 23 January **Julius Zava** of the *Daily News* was assaulted by ZANU-PF supporters and war veterans who were staging a demonstration to protest against the paper's coverage of the assassination of Laurent Kabila, president of the Democratic Republic of Congo. The paper argued that his death was a positive development for Zimbabwe. Although Zava and his colleagues from the *Daily News* were under police protection, demonstrators managed to push through and drag Zava to the ground and kick him. Another journalist from the *Daily News*, **Brian Mangwende**, was threatened during the attack. (RSF, International PEN)

On 26 January three journalists from the *Daily News* and the editor of the *Standard*, **Mark Chavunduka** (*Index* 3/1999, 2/2000, 3/2000. 4/2000), were arrested and questioned by the Criminal Investigative Unit. Deputy editor **Davison Maruziva** and reporters **Conrad Nyamutata** and **Luke Tamborenyoka** were arrested for an article published in October 2000 that maintained that the opposition MDC had filed a civil lawsuit in the US against

ZANU-PF for the political violence that took place in the general elections of June 2000. (MISA, IPI)

Since 27 January supporters of ZANU-PF and war veterans claim to have declared war on the *Daily News*. They confiscated copies of the newspaper and burned them in front of the Zimbabwe Broadcasting Corporation (ZBC) television cameras. In Mutoko they set up a roadblock to search the paper's vehicles and a mob also chased away white patrons and tore up the *Daily News* at the Marondera Country Club. In retaliation, over 150 suspected MDC supporters severely assaulted a driver for the state-owned Zimpapers and left him for dead before burning over 4,000 copies of the state-owned daily *Herald* in Chitungwiza. (MISA, IPI)

On 1 February about 50 war veterans and ZANU-PF supporters besieged the offices of the weekly *Observer* in Mutare and accused publisher **Shadreck Beta**, himself a ZANU-PF official, of publishing articles critical of the government. Beta apologised to the war veterans for anything unethical that might have been written. (MISA)

On 15 February **Mercedes Sayagues**, a Harare-based correspondent for the South African weekly *Mail & Guardian*, was given 24 hours to leave the country after her application to renew her temporary employment permit was refused. Sayagues, a Uruguayan who has lived in Harare since 1992, has written extensively about the corruption, torture and human rights

abuses perpetrated by the ZANU-PF ruling party. On 2 February she reported allegation about the government's involvement in the bombing of the *Daily News*. (MISA, CPJ)

In a similar incident on 17 February, BBC correspondent **Joseph Winter** was asked to leave the country within 24 hours. His work permit had not expired, but was cancelled in unexplained circumstances. He later fled the country as armed police officers were sent to his residence to remove him on 20 February. In deporting both Winter and Sayagues, the government contravened a High Court order which extended the journalists' visas until 23 February. The authorities assured the South African government that the expulsions were not an abuse of press freedom, but claimed that Winter's permit was fraudulent. The BBC claimed that it was valid until February 2002. On 20 February it was reported in the *Herald* that Home Affairs Minister John Nkomo had signed papers prohibiting the return of the two expelled foreign journalists. (MISA, IPI)

Compiled by: Gbenga Oduntan, Shifa Rahman, Polly Rossdale (Africa); Ben Carrdus, Andrew Kendle, Anna Lloyd, Fabio Scarpello (Asia); Louise Finer, Victoria Sams (south and central America); David Gelber, Gill Newsham, Neil Sammonds (Middle East); Humfrey Hunter (north America and Pacific); Claire Fauset (UK and western Europe); Paul Hoffman, Katy Sheppard (eastern Europe and the Balkans)

Greece: Acropolis now

Greece is beginning to reimagine itself. The myths of absolute unity are giving way to a less exclusive vision of nationhood

Acropolis 2000: privates on parade. Credit: © Constantine Manos / Magnum

MARIA MARGARONIS

Fast forward

**A time-lapse film of modern Greece would show a country
shedding its particularity as it comes to terms with the
modern world**

Greece is now – officially – a modern European country. An EEC
member since 1981, it joined the euro in January after Herculean
efforts by the socialist government of Prime Minister Costas Simitis to
make the recalcitrant economy 'converge'. Athens has more cars, more
mobile phones, more people per square metre than almost any other
European city. Yet in every sphere, remnants from the past persist.
Some are physical – crumbling mountain villages up miles of dirt
road, inhabited by goats and a posse of old men. Others are abstract
– the shards of a romantic nationalist ideology formed in the days of
nineteenth-century Balkan nation-building and shattered on the quay
at Smyrna in 1922, when Turkish forces routed the Greek army and
paved the way for a population exchange of nearly two million refugees.

Greece's unique relationship to western Europe – present at the
creation, absent most of the rest of the time – has complicated the part
assigned to it in the West's political narratives. For centuries the region
we now call the Balkans has been Europe's closest 'other' – strikingly
so in the last ten years, when the violence of the Yugoslav war was used
to distance western Europe from its own violent history. Since British
philhellenes set out to free the isles of Greece, western commentators
(and Greeks themselves) have seen the country's Balkan and European
identity as a frustrating puzzle, an impossible either/or.

In the nineteenth century, the debate was about whether modern
Greeks were the descendants of the ancients or a debased 'eastern'
race – swarthy, indolent, not worth the candle. The question resurfaced
in a more modern form in 1993, when Samuel Huntingdon published
an essay, *The Clash of Civilizations?*, outlining the cultural conflict that,

in his view, would replace the Cold War. Though he called his eastern European civilisation 'Slavic-Orthodox', so as to claim the Greece heritage for the West, his map of 'the most significant dividing line in Europe' placed Greece clearly in the east.

Last May, *Time* magazine expressed its surprise at Greece's un-European behaviour in a more demotic vein: 'Twenty terrorist attacks against American targets in a 12-month period; a combined 40 strikes on US, French and British holdings; 52 anti-American protest marches; seven rocket attacks . . . the country in question isn't Afghanistan or Iran. It's Greece. The cradle of democracy, and a key NATO ally, is the home of anti-American terrorism.' The year in question was 1999, when NATO's air war on Yugoslavia provoked mass outrage among Greeks, confirming their reputation as stubborn outsiders. Some of the terrorist attacks were carried out by November 17, a bizarre group which has moved from Marxism-Leninism to ultra-nationalism and which the authorities have spectacularly failed to contain. The more important issue is what lies behind the Greeks' deeper dissent from the western consensus, with which their fate is inextricably bound.

Without a recognition of Greece's Balkan history, it is impossible to understand either the form taken by Greek nationalism or the 'deviations' from European norms that are documented in this issue of *Index*: its attitude to its minorities, or its refusal to separate Church and State even to the degree that they are separate in Britain. The subjects of the Ottoman Empire were identified first by their religion and then by their language, and it was on that basis that they began to organise their national liberation movements. As decentralised peasant societies, they adapted reluctantly to the political models imported from the West. In the course of the nineteenth century, the Enlightenment values of the Greek struggle for independence gave way to irredentism and romantic nationalism.

The western powers also played a highly self-serving role in Greece's war-torn past. The struggle to control the country's strategic position at the crossroads of the eastern Mediterranean has been a critical factor at every stage in its history, from the state's foundation in the nineteenth century, through the Axis occupation and the civil war in the 1940s, to the Colonels' dictatorship of 1967–74, which ended with the Turkish invasion and partition of Cyprus. Greeks tend to see 'the foreign finger' everywhere; its long shadow is very useful to politicians and newspaper owners. But every shadow has its object, however disproportionate in size. (The US State Department also has an infallible talent for feeding Greek paranoia: this February Christos Papoutsakis, founder and editor of *Anti* magazine since 1972, was denied a visa to participate in a panel on 'Dissenting Journalism' at which he was to be Columbia University's guest of honour.)

Of course, explanations are not excuses. The old ideological furniture that clutters up Greek public discourse has been enthusiastically put to use by politicians and others. During the Yugoslav wars, popular support not only for the Serbs but for Slobodan Milosevic was amplified by the media and cheered by political demagogues. Partly a manifestation of a kind of Orthodox nationalism, partly a lightning rod for anti-Americanism of all shades, it also gained momentum from the 'sleaze factor', never to be underestimated in Greek politics. Oil barons and construction kings in the Balkans are tight with media magnates; all of them carefully groom their government connections. The progressive element that saw the bombing of Yugoslavia as an unacceptable imposition of NATO power through violence against civilians was all but lost in the clamour.

There are many in Greece with a vested interest in the climate of hysterical nationalism that has prevailed, with ups and downs, through much of the last decade. No politician has yet confronted it directly. Nevertheless, the last few years have seen the beginning of a new openness. NGOs, research institutions and citizens' groups have formed to work against racism and discrimination of all kinds. A citizens' ombudsman has been appointed to forward concerns to the government. The study of history is shaking off its ideological fetters; books on minority issues are published without difficulty and consumed with interest – among them the Greek translation of Anastasia Karakasidou's *Fields of Wheat, Hills of Blood,* an anthropological study of Greek Macedonia that was cancelled by Cambridge University Press in 1996, after the author had suffered threats, for fear of damaging its interests in Greece.

This openness has been made possible partly by the new experience of 25 years of democratic government, partly by the efforts of the liberal wing of Costas Simitis's government, partly by the moderating influence of European institutions. Though appeals by members of religious and national minorities in Greece to the European Court of Human Rights

Athens, 2000: Gypsy encampment. Credit: Giannis Kampouris

do not always produce concrete results, the fact that such an avenue exists lends authority to their efforts.

Greece's astonishingly swift entry to the single European currency should give some confidence to a nation whose sense of its innate value has gone hand in hand with a feeling of inferiority and subordination. An anecdote from the grim annals of the Roma, perhaps the most despised group in Greece, illustrates the kind of attitude this can produce. Among the many Roma encampments on the edges of Greek towns and cities – some tolerated, but many repeatedly attacked or bulldozed by the authorities – is one of twenty years' standing near a rubbish dump on land belonging to the University of Patras. The university rector recently opposed the installation of a water tap there on the grounds that it would harm the university's reputation: 'What kind of sensitivity can there be towards people who are trespassing on

Athens 2000: ancient and semi-modern.
Credit: Constantine Manos / Magnum

private property, embarrassing the institution internationally when their goats show up in the amphitheatres?' Europe, of course, brings a new set of challenges and problems. Since the end of World War II, Greece has been on a very fast train whose destination is uncertain. If you could make a time-lapse film of the country in that period, you would see thousands of people pouring out of villages; ploughed fields growing over with scrub; forests burning and hotels and shanties blooming in their place. Above all, you would see Athens exploding like a concrete firework, pushing up into an increasingly smog-filled sky and out over the slopes of the mountains that ring it on three sides. At the same time standards of living have risen dramatically. Although Greece is statistically the poorest country in the EU, the life expectancy of its citizens is among the best in the world.

The leap into the single currency has, if possible, accelerated the pace of change. For the first time, Greece has its share of first-world problems. Inflation is down from 22 per cent to less than 3 per cent in ten years and the inefficient public sector is being deregulated. But unemployment is at 13 per cent and rising, homeless people have appeared on the streets, and there is poverty on a new scale, cheek-by-jowl with the plenty. As a final badge of its European identity, Greece has become a country that relies on immigrant labour. Migrants from Albania, Bulgaria, the former Soviet Union, Asia and Africa now make up almost 10 per cent of the population. Their mostly undocumented work has helped to give the economy the extra boost it needed to make it into the Eurozone.

The 2004 Olympic Games, scheduled to take place in Athens despite the fact that few of the athletic facilities are yet complete, are to be the symbol that sells the new Greece to the world. The timing is perfect – a new age, a new revival of Greece's classical (read European) heritage. The old crossroads of the world is being recast as a node in the global nexus of capital. Greece, says an official website, 'aspires to be Europe's strategic link to the emerging markets of the Balkans, the Black Sea, Eastern Europe and the East Mediterranean regions at the dawn of the new millennium'.

There are opportunities here as well as costs. But it is ironic that the modernising forces gradually bringing a greater respect for liberal values also tend to level cultural diversity in favour of the global marketplace. If they are very lucky, some of Greece's speakers of lesser-used languages will be able to join their fellow villagers in making designer olive oil and fine organic cheeses for sale in Athens, Paris and Berlin. In the meantime, just as Greece's new immigrants are pushing it to broaden its sense of itself, perhaps the EU's eastward expansion will pave the way for a wider vision of European identity – one which may finally come to embrace the Balkans. ❏

Maria Margaronis is a correspondent for the Nation. *She would like to thank Leonidas Embiricos and Nafsikaa Papanikolatou for their advice in compiling this file*

MARK MAZOWER

High political stakes

What made the Greeks – and what is unmaking them

The civil war that followed the German occupation of Greece in the 1940s played a huge role in the country's political life for decades to come. What was at stake in that conflict, and why did it take so long for the scars to heal?

The roots of the civil war lay in the crisis of Greek society as it had developed in the previous 20 years and crystallised during the German occupation. At that point you still had a largely nineteenth-century political system with rather clientelistic parties. But society was changing very fast: in the first half of the twentieth century, Greece was becoming an urban country for the first time. The country was also suffering great population pressure: there were 1.5 million refugees after the Asia Minor catastrophe of 1922 who had never been properly dealt with by the state.

Suddenly a new political force emerged during the occupation, which was an organised mass resistance movement led by the previously marginalised Communist Party. The end of the war saw a clash between this great new political force and a traditional political world that had been shaken to its core by the German occupation, and could only now revive itself under British and then American protection, under the banner of saving Greece from communism for the free world.

Eventually the old political elite won out; but it was a very shaky victory. The country was completely destroyed, the state was largely discredited, and it took a long time to rebuild the kind of political, judicial and administrative structures that were necessary for the state to function. What kept this winning side in power for such a long time was simply sustained repression, a more extreme version of the repressive anti-communism that was implicit in the Cold War on the West's side. So Greece lived in this twilight world that was nominally democratic, with a functioning parliament, but in fact was one where the government relied on 'parastate' organisations as much as those of the state, and also institutionalised surveillance of the left.

Can you explain the term 'parastate'?

In Greece, there was a constitutional government from 1952 onwards that looked very democratic. But in practice, there was another layer of legislation that was far more repressive in intent, applied through courts, courts martial, and the military and armed auxiliaries that were connected to the political parties. There was, until the mid-1950s, a fairly large concentration camp population, and many people suspected of coming from the left suffered various disabilities through the 1960s.

The sores of the civil war did not begin to heal until 1974–75, with the end of the Colonels' junta. The dictatorship that held power from 1967 to 1974 was an attempt by certain sections of the right to shore up their defences against what they still saw as the threat from the left. So they were, mentally at least, still fighting the civil war, and indeed a lot of the civil war legislation was still enforced. It was really not until 1974, when the anti-democratic right was discredited as a result of the junta's failures, that the country could begin to move to a fully functioning democratic system.

What are the historical roots of Greece's minorities, and of the majority's attitude towards them?

The Balkans, as we know, had an ethnography that did not lend itself easily to nationalism. The southernmost part of the Balkan peninsula, though, which went on to become independent Greece, is relatively more ethnically homogenous than the rest of the Balkans, by which I mean it is predominantly Christian Orthodox. But it is not, and never was, wholly Christian Orthodox. The outcome of the Greek War of Independence in 1829 was a country for Greeks, by which was meant people who not only spoke Greek but who were Orthodox Christian as well. The war therefore took on something of the character of an ethnic conflict; its very early phases were marked, for instance, by the massacre of the Muslim inhabitants of Tripoli in the Peloponnese.

Once Greece was established as an independent state, it had to reconcile two ostensibly incompatible goals: to set itself up as a modern state, which in the middle of the nineteenth century meant a constitution promising equal rights to all citizens, freedom of religion, freedom of expression, constitutional liberties of various kinds; and to set itself up as a national state for the Greeks. On the whole, the nineteenth century did not go about solving this problem in the way the twentieth century did – namely, getting rid of minorities by killing them. There were some expulsions of minority populations, and there were various disincentives for Muslims to stay, but there was never an actual policy to eject them from the country. Nonetheless, it is striking that the Muslim populations of the main towns dwindled very fast and Muslim landowners sold up and left. There were people, the Catholics or Jews for example, who did not have any other place to move to. And then there was the policy, which we crudely call assimilation, of assuming that minorities will want to move up in the world and become Greek.

After 1912, when Greece acquired its northern provinces in the Balkan Wars, it confronted a much greater ethnographic problem. The Jewish population was preponderant in Salonica, Slavic peasants inhabited many parts of Macedonia, Muslim and Albanian populations occupied much of these areas as well. The country acquired territories that were not obviously Greek, and so the task of making them Greek was a much harder one. The kind of policy implications that were lurking under the surface in the nineteenth century become much more visible in the twentieth century, and of course there were many more wars, more violent and all-consuming than those that had gone before, which tended to acquire ethnic dimensions. World Wars I and II, the Balkan Wars, the two Bulgarian occupations of north-eastern Greece – all these ended up polarising ethnic communities and caused the flight or expulsion of large numbers of minorities or attempts to forcibly assimilate others.

There was, of course, the exchange of populations with Turkey in 1923, which Hellenised the north of Greece in one fell swoop and made the minority groups much less visible.

That's true. At the start of the twentieth century, when Salonika was still an Ottoman city, its population was probably around 140,000, of whom 70,000 were Jews and probably no more than 20,000 were Greek. By 1940, the city's population had more or less doubled to 300,000, but the Jewish population had shrunk to 50,000 and it was well on the way to becoming a Greek city, largely as a result of refugees being settled there.

There is still very much a suspicion in Greece – evidenced in the anxiety a few years ago over the name of the Macedonian republic – that other Balkan countries will try to expand.

To the nationalist, minorities are always a potential fifth column: they are not part of your national community, and the assumption is that they must be part of somebody else's. The attitude to the Slavic minority in northern Greece is a good case in point, but one could also point out the way that Greek Jews have been handled. If you are a historian and you want to look for the documents on Greek Jewry, you would not go, as you might expect, to the Ministry of the Interior, but to the Ministry of Foreign Affairs. I think this speaks volumes about how the Greek state classifies Greek citizens who happen not to be of the Orthodox faith.

The recent wave of immigrants to Greece from Albania and the former Yugoslavia has met with a pretty hostile reception. Can you explain why?

Greece came to see itself in the twentieth century as a country of emigration. There was huge transatlantic emigration before World War I and, particularly to Germany, after World War II. So the idea that Greece is now sufficiently wealthy to attract people of its own – and sufficiently prosperous to be suffering labour shortages – required a readjustment in people's attitudes, which took quite a time. One can see exactly the same thing happening in Italy and Spain. I think it is interesting that there is now quite a lot of discussion and debate in the Greek media about the implications of this. Many Greeks are now asking themselves: 'Are we a multicultural society? Should we become one? Is this compatible with Hellenism?'

In your book Dark Continent *you write: 'Europeans accept democracy because they no longer believe in politics.' Do you think that is or could be true of the Greeks?*

I don't think that it is true of Greece, actually. I don't think it is true of those parts of Europe that have gone through fierce political conflict, and that have known the meaning of high political stakes.

A lot has changed in Greece: there is a general suspicion of ideology, and in that sense the country is part of a common European trend. It is quite interesting that a lot of new historical research is being done into the children of partisans, for example, which shows pretty clearly that on the one hand they are quite proud of their parents, but on the other are very critical of them for sacrificing their children and their family cohesion to ideological struggle. The idea of an all-pervasive commitment to the struggle, whether it is communist or nationalist, has really gone. But there is still a sense of a national project and a threat to the national project. People are very aware of being a weak country and of the overwhelming strength of the USA. There is still a lot of anti-Americanism in Greece, which is understandable when you think of the power America exerted in Greece during and after the civil war. There is still a fear of Turkey and there are still clashes between the two countries – Greek–Turkish relations remain unresolved. So there are still things to play for in a way that may not seem so obvious in other European countries. ❏

Mark Mazower *is Anniversary Professor of History at Birkbeck College, London. His most recent book is the edited collection* After the War Was Over: Reconstructing the Family, Nation and State in Greece, 1943–1960 *(Princeton University Press). Interview by Maria Margaronis*

TASOULA VERVENIOTI

Nails and water

Many who fought in the resistance against the German occupation of Greece and in the civil war that followed were persecuted for decades after, regardless of their politics. It is only recently that they have felt free to tell their stories

Lisika Theodoridou-Sozopoulou's parents came to northern Greece in the exchange of populations with Turkey that came a year after the Asia Minor disaster of 1922.

> I was born in 1925 in the village of Tsoumas, in the prefecture of Kozani. Tsoumas is a Turkish name because, before the refugees, Turks lived there. The refugees arrived in 1922 and the village was named Amigdala [Almonds] and, a little later, Haravgi [Dawn].

Lisika's mother pushed her to study. She got into secondary school but then the Germans invaded. With most of the village, her family joined the massive popular resistance movement EAM (the National Liberation Front), a coalition of many groups dominated by the Communist Party. On 2 January 1944 the Germans and their Greek collaborators surrounded the village, plundered and burned the houses of EAM members and arrested her older brother. Then her father took 18-year-old Lisika to 'the Mountain', to Free Greece. She joined the partisans and became a second lieutenant of ELAS, the National People's Liberation Army. During the period known as the White Terror that followed the German withdrawal, anyone who had taken part in the resistance with EAM was at risk of prosecution.

> After the Liberation we were in danger all day long . . . I wanted to leave, but I didn't because I wanted to get my secondary school diploma. I went to take the exams in 1946. I was good at maths but I failed the essay. The subject was 'What are the ideals of youth?' I wrote the ideals of EPON (EAM's youth wing) and they

Lisika Theodoridou-Sozopoulou.
Credit: *Johanna Weber, from* Faces of the Greek
Resistance – Memory of Death, Memory of
Life *(Agra Press, 1996)*

failed me . . . In 1946–47 I
was a student at the secondary
school again, but they watched
my every step. They would
call me to the police station for
no reason . . . The headmaster
looked at me like a dog. Then I
felt old . . . I'd stand in front of
the mirror and look at myself
and say: 'Is that you, Lisika?
Why don't you laugh? Why
can't you laugh?' That beautiful,
spontaneous, childish laugh was
gone.

Lisika was arrested at dawn on
14 January 1948, tortured and
brought before the Special Martial
Law Court of Kozani. She was released but, on 25 March, the national
holiday, she was asked to make a speech in the village square denouncing
EAM and the Communist Party. She refused and was arrested 'as a
precaution' and sent into internal exile until 1951. She met her future
husband in prison; they were married in 1954.

> I never got my secondary school diploma. When I came out
> of exile, I needed 30 drachmas for the stamp and I didn't have it.
> Everything was closed to us. The Golgotha of survival was terribly
> difficult for second-class Greeks, as they called us. There was no
> work anywhere either for me or for my husband. The only thing
> they couldn't deny us was the earth, the soil we dig with our nails
> and water with our sweat. During the dictatorship, they didn't
> forget us. They hunted my husband down and he ran away from
> the village and was lost in an accident.

Sasha Tsakiri was born in Athens to conservative parents and joined
the Resistance while studying at Athens University. In the spring of
1944 she met Kiriakos Tsakiris, a cadre of the Communist Youth and a
founder member of EPON. They were married in June.

I went back to university after the Liberation, in 1945 . . . In May or June, Kiriakos got the order [from the party] to leave Athens . . . and I got a telegram – 'Come at once!' I abandoned my studies and went to the country with him to be his cover, because he couldn't go out . . . In the summer of 1947 he left for the Mountain. I said goodbye to him and, when I got home, I started crying and I said, 'My life is over.'

When did you meet again?

In 1966. On 30 April, Kiriakos was released. Exactly a year later, the dictatorship came and they arrested him and another five years went by . . . We never had a child. I had an abortion when Kiriakos had to go to the Mountain. I didn't on any account want to have a child that would be brought up by other people.

Kiriakos died two years ago. Sasha lives in Athens.

Evdokia, later Vera Foteva, was born in Dendrochori in the prefecture of Kastoria. She was Macedonian. She learned Greek at primary school. The teacher persuaded her mother to send her to secondary school in Kastoria.

When I went to the secondary school the other girls treated me very badly. 'You dirty Bulgarian! What are you here for?' I just swallowed it and carried on. I was a good student. When the war started my mother couldn't stand it any more, because I was her only daughter . . . and I went back to the village.

The village had suffered during the persecution of Slav speakers under the Metaxas dictatorship. During the war a communist cell was organised and Evdokia joined the Communist Youth, and later the Communist Party and the Slavo-Macedonian People's Liberation Front. From September 1943 she lived underground and took the pseudonym Vera, which she has kept ever since. She was secretary of the Slavophone women of the whole region. When a Macedonian battalion was formed in the ranks of ELAS, she became a partisan. But by the end of the occupation a rift had opened between Greek-speaking and Slav-speaking communists:

We were setting an ambush for the Germans. And up behind us
comes Keravnos's battalion. He was from the villages near Florina,
we knew each other well. He came up behind us to fire on us.
We're going to fire on the Germans and they're coming behind
us to fire on us . . . That was – what can I say? We came here [to
Yugoslavia]. Where could we go? ELAS was going to fire on us
from every side. Later we united again. Together again.

During the civil war, Tito split with Stalin. After their defeat, fighters
of the Democratic Army (ELAS's successor) crossed to Albania.

Outside Elbasa, a jeep comes along and an officer hands me
a blue envelope . . . I open it: 'Comrade Vera, you, Minas and
Urania must come at once to General Headquarters. [When we
get there] he gives me a blank piece of paper. 'Write about your
treachery,' he says. I said, 'I don't know which of us is a traitor . . .'
Then they took us to Tirana . . . We were in cells, separately, for
almost three months . . . One night they put us on a lorry and
took us to Dirachio. We thought they were going to kill us. They
brought us to the ship, all in one room on the floor, and took us
to Odessa. On 25 December they took us to the Odessa prison
and, on New Year's Day, they put us on a prison train and took
us to Moscow. My husband was saying on the ship: 'Oh, we're
in the Soviet Union. There are no prisons.'

From the Moscow prisons they were sent in 1952 to a camp in
Irkutsk, Siberia, and, in 1955, exiled to Alma Ata. When Stalin died
they managed to leave and, via Belgrade, reached Skopje, where Vera
still lives.

We didn't feel like foreigners. We felt that we lived in Greece, but
we were not Greeks. We were born there. We were not foreigners
. . . It is hard to be in a foreign country. Our homeland is there
[in Greek Macedonia], and now I can't go there. You can't take
one flower to put on the grave of those who were killed there.
They are down there. Not one flower. Why? ❏

Tasoula Vervenioti is the author of I Gynaika tis Antistasis: I eisodos ton
gynaikon stin politiki *(Odysseas, Athens), a study of women in the wartime
resistance. Translated by Maria Margaronis*

HELENA SMITH

Clerics in uniform

The struggle between traditionalists and modernisers has found a focus in the unfinished row about what should be written on Greek citizens' ID cards

In the very hot summer of 2000, after hundreds of thousands of demonstrators had taken to the streets in protest over the move to drop the religion affiliation from state ID cards, I sat down to write a piece about Greece's identity crisis. The prospect was not particularly alluring: if anything, it filled me with trepidation. In the autumn of 1993 I had received several death threats – as sophisticated in their high-tech delivery as they were in quiet menace – for daring to mention in print the feeble health of the late prime minister, Andreas Papandreou. Although perturbed, officials were also perplexed. Why hadn't I just indulged in a bit of self-censorship?

'You had an interview with Mr Papandreou and abused the privilege by writing about his frail voice and rouged cheeks,' snarled Teti Georgantopoulou, the socialist leader's agitated press secretary, hauling me into her office. 'Tell me, what are these things you see and hear that nobody else does? The prime minister is most healthy. Such articles hurt Greece and moreover they are very rude.'

Worse was to come. In the winter of 1994 a seemingly innocuous story penned from Thessaloniki on the country's burgeoning north–south divide caused such a commotion that the mass-selling daily *Eleftheros Typos* saw fit to proclaim on its front page that 'The *Guardian* and the Foreign Office are carving up our country.' Again, the powers that be were none too pleased. In Athens, the word was out to keep 'the English spy and mis-Hellene' at arm's length.

No event so neatly sums up Greece's political landscape – or its transition from a Balkan backwater into a modern European state – as the ongoing crisis over the ID cards. In more ways than one, it has come

Archbishop Christodoulos of Athens.
Credit: Thanasis Dimopoulos

to symbolise Greece's growing pains. It came as some surprise, then, that the reaction to my articles about the row – sparked by the socialist government's desire to comply with EU standards – was anything but explosive. To be sure, there were the predictable outbursts of anger from nationalists and the Greek Orthodox Church, the self-styled protector of Hellenism. 'Our faith is the foundation of our identity. If you abolish one, you abolish the other,' Archbishop Christodoulos, the country's spiritual leader, had told protestors. Allow for the deletion of religion from the cards – first introduced by a military dictatorship in the 1930s – and, he thundered, it would mean the end of the Balkans' only homogenous state. (Greece has been repeatedly condemned by the European Court of Human Rights for violations against its Jewish, Catholic and Muslim minorities.) For the Greek Church, whose influence remains supreme, the measure was tantamount to a plot to de-Hellenise the nation. My own views, according to the Holy Synod, author of an especially venomous epistle now accessible on the Church's website, were equal to the worst kind of communist propaganda.

But, this time, the response on the part of the Greek press and the ruling socialist party was subtle and low-key. Greece had changed. In some small measure, the powers that had taken such offence just a few years before were speaking another language: the global lingo of increased openness that has accompanied the country's inevitable integration with the rest of the West. This time, there would be no official complaints.

From its inception, the ID card quarrel has marshalled modernisers against traditionalists – the retrograde forces still resisting change in the one European country to have experienced neither a widespread Renaissance nor an Industrial Revolution. What should have been a minor, almost unnoticed reform has unexpectedly become a fiery national issue – one that has caused clerics, housewives and neo-Orthodox intellectuals to speak publicly of a brewing 'civil war'. Not since the nationalist outbursts in the early 1990s over the name of Macedonia has Greece's culture of intolerance been so starkly exposed. All at once, it seemed, the country's political fault-lines were on display, pitting its liberal, civic-minded and cosmopolitan elite (exemplified by both Prime Minister Costas Simitis and Foreign Minister George Papandreou) against the parochial, paranoid and anti-western forces of Christodoulos and the Turk-hating, minority-loathing, immigrant-bashing 'super-patriot' purists whose support he enjoys.

Fearing a blow to their formidable power base, the clerics show no sign of backing down. For the past six months, they have waged a concerted campaign to collect signatures for an 'informal referendum' on the issue. Such is their hunger for names that they gather them quite unabashedly at funerals and weddings. A friend of mine was recently pressed into signing such a petition only minutes after burying his mother on the Aegean island of Limnos.

Unlike so many other splits in Greece's tumultuous modern history, this one does not run neatly between left and right. Indeed, what makes Archbishop Christodoulos's appeal so potent is its ability to cross party lines. Symbolising as it does the ever-present tug-of-war over Greece's embrace of Europe, the ID card debacle has been used by the spiritual leader to address all those who fear change the most: those who have been worst hit by the demands of a global economy and government cutbacks in the bloated state sector; and those who see the Church as the embodiment of Greece's defensive national identity. A televangelist *par excellence*, Christodoulos has drawn his support from a heady mix of the marginalised petit bourgeoisie, unskilled workers, disgruntled civil servants and the small-time self-employed – people who have seen their purchasing power cut in half because of punishing, EU-dictated economic reforms. To many of the archbishop's supporters, the Church is the only bulwark left against the threat of a multicultural, open society, symbolised for them by the yuppies who work for multinationals, drive jeeps and wield mobiles like firearms.

The rapidity of change as Athens joins the single European currency is only likely to deepen the discontent. Although Greece has long felt the cultural effects of globalisation (evidenced by the American soaps on television and the foreign words that pepper everyday speech), major economic and educational restructuring has yet to come. And sadly there are still politicians within Pasok, the governing Panhellenic Socialist Movement, who are only too willing to use the popular malaise to score points. When the crisis erupted, Evangelos Venizelos, the French-trained former justice minister, unexpectedly sided with the Church. 'Greece is going through its own version of *Death of a Salesman*,' says Nikiforos Diamantouros, the country's ombudsman and a political scientist. 'The voices of protest will become shriller and shriller as these traditionally minded eastern Greeks begin to see their historic end.'

On a political level the discontent is being mirrored in a culture of distrust, not least around the government's ground-breaking, reform-minded policies in foreign affairs. Although efforts at rapprochement with NATO ally Turkey have met with approval, growing numbers of Greeks are beginning to feel they may have gone too far – criticism that has been happily echoed by Theodore Pangalos, the pugnacious former foreign minister who, for political expediency, has also lined up with the anti-western bloc. Similarly, there is mounting disaffection with the socialists' change of tack in the Balkans, where Greece is the sole EU member. Its shift of support from the Milosevic regime to the democratic opposition in the run-up to the Yugoslav election has increasingly been the butt of criticism, despite being widely credited by the West and boosting Greece's standing in the region.

In recent months the attacks have come to focus on George Papandreou's chief strategist Alex Rondos, a brilliant, Oxford-educated, diaspora Greek. As a man now cast by traditionalists as the 'dangerous outsider', Rondos, perhaps more than anyone else, can be seen as a barometer of Greece's identity crisis. His presence in Athens is a measure of Prime Minister Simitis's desire to take risks and embrace reform; his departure would signal retrenchment. Whether men like Rondos stay the course will indicate how fast Greece will move, as a truly multicultural civil society, into the future. It will also say a lot about the country's ability to resolve the identity crisis that has plagued it, in one way or another, from its birth as a modern state. ❏

Helena Smith holds a Nieman Fellowship at Harvard University, awarded for her coverage of Greece and the Balkans as the Athens-based correspondent for the Guardian *and* Observer

LAMBROS BALTSIOTIS & LEONIDAS EMBIRICOS

Speaking in tongues

The battle over minority languages hots up

On 2 February this year, a criminal court in Athens passed a 15-month jail sentence on Sotiris Bletsas, an architect and promoter of the Vlach language, effectively ruling that no language other than Greek is spoken by citizens today. Bletsas's 'crime' was distributing a leaflet produced by the European Bureau for Lesser-Used Languages – a body linked with the EU – at an annual gathering of Vlachs in 1995. The leaflet listed all the lesser-used languages of Europe, including those spoken in Greece: in its terminology, Arvanite, Aroumanian (Vlach), Bulgarian (by Pomaks), Slav-Macedonian and Turkish.

Kimi, in the Rhodope mountains: Pomak girls in the primary school.
Credit: Lambris Baltsiotis

Multicultural package tour

The only large non-Greek-speaking group within the original borders of the Greek kingdom in 1830 was the **Arvanites**. They spoke a language descended from medieval Albanian and actively participated from the start in the imagined community of the Greek nation. The use of their language is sharply declining, but it is still spoken in parts of southern Greece. Any attempt to revive Arvanitika has now been quashed by the communities' desperate efforts to distance themselves from the Albanian immigrants arriving since 1991.

The **Aroumanians** or **Vlachs**, who speak a Balkan Romance language, became part of the Greek state with its northward expansions in 1881 and 1912–13. Their political importance outweighed their numbers because they were represented in the upper echelons of every Balkan elite, and because their Greek orientation offered Greece a foothold in solidly Slav-speaking areas. The Vlachs maintain an impressive array of networks and cultural organisations. There is no mass demand for the preservation of the language; instead, there is a loose community bound together by a sense of linguistic and cultural identity and ethnic pride unique in the Greek context.

The annexation of Macedonia by Greece in 1912–13 brought a large number of **Slav-speaking Christians** under Greek control – then the largest single population in a region that was claimed by Serbia and Bulgaria. The limited number of Greek-speakers compelled Greece to conceal the truth about the area's linguistic composition. A policy of harsh treatment to suppress the Slav language and force the population to assimilate was intensified and formalised. Between 1913 and 1927 part of the population left for, or were exchanged with, Bulgaria. During World War II a substantial portion turned towards Bulgaria; another large portion then joined the Greek Resistance movement EAM, where it flirted with the Yugoslav form of Macedonian nationalism. The bitterness of that episode still festers. In 1982, when the PASOK government welcomed back the political refugees who had left during the civil war, it cruelly denied (and still denies) the right of return, even for a brief visit, to all those who were 'not Greek by origin' – for which read Slavophones, regardless of national affiliation.

It is difficult to gauge what proportion of Slav-speakers would now identify as nationally Macedonian. In the European elections of 1994 the

Macedonian Rainbow Party won at least 7,000 votes, but there are certainly more people with a Macedonian identity who would not go as far as voting for the Rainbow (the party was prosecuted, and acquitted, in 1998 for 'inciting dissent' by putting up a sign in Macedonian outside its offices in Florina in 1995).

The Albanian-speaking **Tchams** of western Epirus also came under Greek jurisdiction in 1913. The Christian part of this population identified with the Greek state, but the approximately 20,000 Muslims were violently forced to leave for Albania at the end of World War II, after collaborating with the occupiers.

Most of the Muslim population of Greece was exchanged in the 1920s with the Orthodox population of Turkey. A substantial number of these Orthodox refugees were Turkish-speaking; some still are. The **Muslims of western Thrace**, who were exempt from this exchange, were made up of two major groups, the **Turks** and the **Pomaks**, who speak a dialect of Bulgarian. While the proportion of Pomaks to Turks steadily grows as the latter emigrate, the Pomaks themselves increasingly adopt not only the Turkish language but a Turkish national identity, mainly because of the historical prestige of Turkish Muslim culture. Though discrimination by the state has lessened, the authorities have done little to dismantle local power structures that perpetuate it. Progress is stalled both by the state and by the intense nationalism of part of the minority, which has contributed over the past ten years to its continuing ghettoisation. The belated repeal of discriminatory laws – the abolition of a statute allowing for the removal of minority citizens' Greek nationality in 1998, the lifting of a ban on entry to the minority's mountain region in 1995 – do not represent a profound change in policy. Unconstitutional laws are still in effect, restricting among other things the free expression of minority teachers, and education remains a problem.

The largest minority-language community today is that of the **Roma**, who face severe problems of social exclusion. There is also the remnant of a large historic **Jewish** community, mainly Spanish-speaking Sephardim, which was almost destroyed by the Holocaust, and a small community of **Armenians**. In the past, Greek **Catholics** faced some discrimination, but their situation is gradually improving. ❏

LB & LE

Two prosecution witnesses testified that they themselves speak Vlach, while the New Democracy MP who brought the case acknowledged that his grandparents (refugees from Asia Minor) spoke only Turkish. Yet the court convicted Bletsas of 'disseminating false information' which could 'provoke public anxiety and give the impression that there are minority problems in Greece'. The prosecutor referred to language as 'a factor that shapes national consciousness, a racial criterion', while the judge herself, conceding that other 'idioms' (but not languages!) are spoken in Greece, doubted whether 'we ought to be talking about it'.

This judgment is a sharp reminder of how deeply rooted the fear of linguistic and religious difference is in Greece. It comes at a time when we believed that the extreme nationalist intolerance of the early 1990s had finally subsided. But in spite of a liberalisation in the government's approach to minorities and 'national issues' under prime minister Costas Simitis, the discussion of minority languages, let alone of national minorities, remains taboo.

For instance, in June 2000 a conference organised by KEMO (the Minority Groups Research Centre) to discuss the Council of Europe's Charter of Minority and Regional Languages was cancelled after backstage interventions from middle- and low-ranking officials of the ministry of foreign affairs (which is responsible for minority issues in Greece) and from within the Vlach-speaking community. Greece and Turkey are the only members of the Council where there has been no public meeting to discuss the Charter and its ratification. The press hushed up the matter, but a number of New Democracy MPs tabled parliamentary questions about the 'suspicious' conference and demanded explanations from the government.

Two years earlier, a conference about the Vlach language, organised by KEMO in Larisa with partial EU funding, was shut down by protesters. The main regional newspaper ran a front-page story about the conference, making the obviously absurd claim that 'the question of a Vlach state will probably be raised'. 'Indignant citizens' stormed the hotel, heckled the participants and stopped the proceedings. For some time afterwards, the organisers were described as 'traitors' and 'foreign agents' in the media and a series of questions about them were tabled in parliament by New Democracy MPs.

In the past 20 years, Greece's historical suspicion of its non-Greek speaking and non-Orthodox citizens has been cultivated by both major parties for their own political ends. The existence of the Turkish minority in western Thrace, and of a Slavophone population in Greece (not to mention a Macedonian national minority) were the two great secrets kept by the Greek state until the end of the 1980s – a decade in which the ruling socialist party fostered a heady atmosphere of populist nationalism.

The PASOK government, while healing the wounds of the civil war and broadening civil rights in general, adopted harsh policies towards the Turkish minority, in some cases almost rivalling those of the junta. Administrative harassment and steady discrimination pushed the minority to emigrate, but also radicalised most of its members around the issue of their Turkish identity, which is forbidden expression. (This minority – the only one officially recognised in Greece – is acknowledged only as a 'Muslim minority'.) The response was a 'small pogrom' in 1990, carried out by more 'indignant citizens' in the town of Komotini with the shocking collusion, if not the encouragement, of the authorities. The Greek media suppressed all reports of these events.

Komotini, 30 January 1990: riot police march through the old market.
Credit: Constantine Tsiselikis

The election of the conservative New Democracy in 1990 brought some relaxation of policy in Thrace, but also locked Greece once again into its long-established attitude of suspicion towards its northern neighbours. The tensions of those years were exploited by almost all the print and electronic media. With the deterioration of relations with Turkey and the emergence of the Republic of Macedonia, the 'non-existent' Turkish and Macedonian minorities were portrayed by populist means as fifth columnists, and their members were subjected to a series of trials and convictions. For example, Ahmet Sadik, an Independent MP from western Thrace, served two months in prison in 1991 for 'spreading false information' because he collected signatures on a petition of protest about the minority's situation and for 'inciting dissent' because he used the terms Turk and Turkish about the minority and its members. Minority journalists were convicted on the same charges.

Activists from the Macedonian community also faced violations of their right of association. A routine application to found a 'House of Macedonian Culture' was rejected in 1994; though the 'House' won an appeal before the European Court of Human Rights, no lawyer in its home town of Florina has yet agreed to file the necessary papers with the courts. In 1993 the logo of a Macedonian magazine in Edessa was refused recognition, and two Macedonians were prosecuted simply for claiming that there is a Macedonian minority and that it faces discrimination.

Greece evidently still feels threatened by the presence of a Slavo-phone population, some of whom do not identify as Greek (though not all of them would necessarily identify as Macedonian). The reason for this fear is not numbers or political weight, but the implications the community could acquire in relation to the historical 'Macedonian Question'. The fear that a Macedonian national identity could extend to the whole linguistic, geographical and social continuum that makes up the Slavophone community in Greece runs very deep – as evidenced in Greece's panic over the name of the Republic of Macedonia when it became independent in 1991. Such was the paranoia over this issue that members of leftist organisations were given prison sentences simply for supporting recognition of the former Yugoslav republic.

The extraordinary hostility of the press, elected officials and much of the public towards the slightest deviation from the 'norm' of the Greek-speaking Orthodox Greek can only be understood by going back to the nineteenth century, when the young state's ideological arsenal against rival (and later) nationalisms took shape. The ancient Greek language and its prestige had great importance for the foundation of modern Greece. The appeal of the Greek language and Greek education were the basis on which the country expanded to the north, annexing territories that were also being claimed – with a real chance of success – by other Balkan nations.

Since then, linguistic and ethnic difference has formed the basis for the 'geopolitical insecurity' still rampant in governing circles, which has also taken root in a large part of the population. (This is, in some cases, understandable: about a fifth of the population is descended from Greek refugees from Turkey, Bulgaria, Russia and the former Soviet Union, while eastern Macedonia and western Thrace suffered at least two harsh occupations and annexations by Bulgaria in the last century.) The concept of an Orthodox 'nation', which derives from the Ottoman *Millet*, was used to claim Orthodox non-Greek speakers – a large population in what is now northern Greece – for the new Greek nation. This notion of a religious 'nation' meant that Greece had great difficulty embracing Greek Catholics, let alone Jews or Muslims. The romantic nationalist narrative of Greek history from classical times onwards was also disseminated in these new regions, creating a rationale for the obliteration of other languages – established policy since 1880.

Given the level of national integration in Greece today, discriminatory policies and attitudes that were considered acceptable by nation states from the nineteenth century until the middle of the twentieth are unjustifiable, and create problems not only for citizens but for the state itself. Although historical difference still bears a great symbolic weight, it now has much less political importance than the issue of Greece's new immigrants. ❏

Lambros Baltsiotis is a lawyer and historian. Leonidas Embiricos is a historian. They are both members of KEMO (the Minority Groups Research Centre). Translated by Maria Margaronis

PANAYOTE ELIAS DIMITRAS

Anyone who feels Turkish

'In Greece there are no ethnic media since the Greek nation is unified. It is unique in Europe in being 100 per cent homogeneous . . . In Greece, regions of ethnic tension or conflict do not exist'—*Journalists' Union of Athens Daily Newspapers, 1999*

In late July 1999, for the first time in Greece's history, there was a short-lived debate on the country's minority and citizenship policies. It was triggered by an appeal for the recognition of a Macedonian and a Turkish minority, and for the unconditional ratification by parliament of the Council of Europe's Framework Convention for the Protection of National Minorities. The appeal was signed by the (then) three Turkish minority deputies in parliament, as well as three Macedonians, seven Turkish and three human rights NGOs, and was announced on the 25th anniversary of the end of the Colonels' dictatorship.

Without exception, Greece's mainstream political parties fell over each other to condemn the document. Parliamentary Speaker Apostolos Kaklamanis, of the governing PASOK Party, said: 'It is well known that in Greece there is no Turkish or Macedonian minority. There is a Muslim religious minority, which is respected. Any inventions that serve other purposes will be handled in the appropriate way.' Deputy Foreign Minister Gregory Niotis argued that 'the text is based on subjective absurdities and unfounded opinions'. Defence Minister Akis Tsohatzopoulos spoke of 'fantasies'. The official spokesman of the conservative New Democracy Party, Aris Spiliotopoulos, commented: 'Groundless and vacuous arguments . . . referring to the existence of national minorities in Greece, have no relation to reality. Attempts to artificially distort the truth and the democratic situation prevailing today throughout the country are rejected by all Greek citizens, regardless of their religious beliefs.'

Two parties of the left were even shriller in their efforts to prove their patriotism. Communist Party leader Aleka Papariga called the appeal 'more than odd and hardly innocent' and added that 'it gives the US the opportunity to impose their conditions on the [Greek–Turkish] dialogue'. Dimitris Tsovolas, leader of the socialist splinter party DIKKI, described the appeal as 'an insolent provocation that stains the 25th anniversary of the restoration of democracy in our country . . . Such unacceptable, provocative, unhistorical actions are part of Turkish propaganda and of other anti-Greek circles.'

With the exception of one leftist daily, all 21 national newspapers reacted to the appeal with hysteria and hostility. 'Raw provocation by three deputies for a Turkish minority' shouted the largest-selling daily *Ta Nea* which, in its editorial, accused the deputies and the human rights NGOs of wanting to 'spark a minority problem' on the orders of Ankara. Its main competitor, *Eleftherotypia*, ran an article by a Greek-American academic who identified the hand of 'Ankara and its patrons in Washington, with the support of the human rights industry in the US and its affiliates in Greece' behind the document. The third largest paper, *To Ethnos*, carried the front-page headline 'Turkish bomb on the Anniversary' and called the deputies a Turkish 'fifth column' and 'traitors' with an 'allegiance to foreign masters'. The staid conservative *Kathimerini*, considered the most authoritative of Greek papers, bore the headline 'Suspicious provocation'. It bolstered its argument that the appeal came from 'obscure' sources 'playing the game of Ankara's nationalist circles' by claiming that the three minority deputies denied any knowledge of it, in spite of the fact that all three were appearing on private television channels confirming and explaining their signature. The paper never bothered to retract its story, which all the state media picked up and repeated several times.

The intellectuals' silence was deafening. Only two minor extreme-left groups publicly backed the appeal. On the other hand, a leading academic who has chaired the only university department in Greece with a graduate programme in human rights announced: 'Anyone who feels Turkish should move to Turkey.'

A few days later, Foreign Minister George Papandreou dared to hint that Greece may finally move towards the application of the

internationally accepted norms for national minorities and the
recognition of the right to self-identification for Macedonians and Turks.
He said: 'If a Greek citizen feels that he belongs to some ethnic group,
international treaties allow this. And Greece is a country that respects
international agreements . . . No one challenges the fact that there are
[in Greece] many Muslims of Turkish origin. Of course, the treaties
[governing the 1923 exchange of populations] refer to Muslims. If the
borders are not challenged, it concerns me little if someone calls himself
a Turk, a Bulgarian or a Pomak . . . Also, whoever feels he has a
[Macedonian] origin, Greece has nothing to fear from it and I want to
stress this is not just my thinking. It is a well-established practice that
allows the integration of minorities throughout Europe, as well as in
other countries like Canada, Australia and the USA. Such an attitude
defuses whatever problems might have existed, allows the real
blossoming of democratic institutions and also gives these people the
feeling that they too are citizens of this country.'

The editorial in *To Vima*, the country's leading opinion-making
newspaper, summarised the backlash that followed, which included calls
by PASOK MPs for Papandreou's dismissal: 'There could not be even one
Greek citizen, however conciliatory, ready even to discuss the presence
of racial minorities. The Greek people is one and indivisible . . . The
government should immediately rectify a lapse, even involuntary,
that gives rise to obvious and less obvious dangers.' The Framework
Convention was never sent to parliament for ratification and, a year
later, Papandreou, grooming himself as a potential prime minister,
had changed his tune: 'Our position is that, according to the Council
of Europe's Convention, which we have signed and will ratify in
parliament, "minority" is a legal term . . . Every country's government
has the right to define which minority it recognises. We recognise as
a minority the Muslim minority. This does not mean that we do not
acknowledge that there are some Slav-speakers in our country. They
are not a minority in the legal sense. A minority in the legal sense has
consequences concerning its rights, eg schools, or whatever. Secondly,
we recognise this minority as Muslim. This does not mean, however,
that there is no individual right to define oneself: "I have Turkish roots,
so I am a Turk," "I am a Pomak," etc.'

Never mind that all elected leaders of the 'Muslim minority' claim
its right to be recognised as Turkish – or that, in 1995, an EU survey

'Turks to Turkey'. Credit: © Nikos Ecnomopoulos / Magnum

recorded that 80 per cent of the minority's members identified themselves as Turkish, while only 10 per cent considered themselves Greek. Most intergovernmental and NGO human rights reports critical of Greece go unreported in the media – which is eager to quote the same sources at length when they issue reports critical of Turkey. Faced with such overwhelming propaganda, most Greeks end up believing that they live in a near-perfect democracy. Some may admit that there is intolerance towards immigrants, and will report and debate on EU-wide surveys that register the highest percentage of xenophobia in Greece. But when Macedonian or Turkish activists report on human rights violations, they are met with silence or hostility. ❏

Panayote Elias Dimitras *is a spokesperson for Greek Helsinki Monitor and a visiting lecturer at the Central European University*

MICHAEL HOWARD

Diversity of propaganda

**The furore caused by the use of depleted uranium in former
Yugoslavia also exposed dangerously depleted levels of
impartiality in the media**

January 2001 should have been a triumphant time for Greece. The
government of Prime Minister Costas Simitis had completed the
Sisyphean task of pushing the economy up the slopes of convergence
to arrive in Europe's inner sanctum. Relations with age-old rival Turkey,
which reached a nadir two years ago after Athens' bungled attempt
to shelter the Kurdish leader Abdullah Ocalan, were slowly improving;
and the country had earned praise from the international community
for its 'positive' engagement in the Balkans, in particular its mediating
role during the peaceful change of regime in Belgrade last autumn.

Perhaps the time had come to shrug off the anxieties and insecurities
of the post-Cold War era, when Greece adopted a series of surreal
foreign policy positions – most notably its hysteria over the name
of the Macedonian Republic and its support for Slobodan Milosevic.
It was time to approach the world outside with more self-confidence.
Yet despite a government publicity blitz, the historic step that took
Greece into the single currency left the public largely unmoved.
Another matter diverted their gaze and, fanned by an irrepressibly
nationalist media, plunged the country back into the uncertainty that
plagued south-eastern Europe throughout the 1990s. Depleted uranium.

This posed a dilemma for the government. As reports of cases of
leukaemia among veterans of the Bosnian and Kosovo wars spread, many
of Greece's 1,500-strong peacekeeping contingent in Kosovo asked to be
posted home. Athens had opted out of the NATO bombing of Yugoslavia
amid overwhelming domestic opposition, but set much store by its

contribution to the international peacekeeping force. It stood to lose face among its NATO allies if it couldn't keep its contingent up to strength. Defence Minister Akis Tsochadzopoulos appealed for level-headedness. 'I think what is important is for the facts to be made known, and not to have hysteria and emotion take over,' he said. His words fell on deaf ears.

Concern and anger over NATO's use of depleted uranium ordnance was not confined to Greece. But the way the story was reported here scuppered any possibility of serious debate. Though there is no conclusive proof linking exposure to depleted uranium with leukaemia, NATO and the West were summarily tried and found guilty by the Greek press. A few examples provide a flavour of the coverage. Over a picture of a mother holding a deformed baby, *Eleftherotypia*, the second biggest daily, ran a headline 'Here's the innocent uranium' (in Greek, 'NATO' also means 'here is the'). The subhead read: 'Shock: nightmarish documents from bombings against civilians.' *Ta Nea*, the market leader, ran with 'THEY KNEW for four years that uranium causes cancer – secret report by British army kept hidden.' 'In cold blood' screamed the conservative *Adesmeftos Typos*. 'Shocking documents reveal those guilty of nuclear nightmare in Greece,' it continued. *Athinaiki*, meanwhile, recruited both the terrible Turk and the Cyprus imbroglio into the DU debate: 'Revelation! Occupied Cyprus is warehouse for uranium bombs.'

One of the most breathtaking comments appeared in the left-wing *Avghi*. Professor Aliki Yotopoulos-Marangopoulos, president of the National Human Rights Commission of Greece declared: 'In my lifetime, I have twice felt ashamed to be a human being: first when Nazi crimes were revealed at the end of World War II, and today with the revelations about uranium bombs in neighbouring Yugoslavia.' This statement from the country's leading human rights official may have been made in the heat of the moment, but it gelled with the message being peddled by the majority of journalists, intellectuals and politicians: the use of DU was evidence that the 'great powers' or 'evil West' were once again trying to subjugate the Orthodox peoples of south-eastern Europe. 'Greeks are an emotional lot,' explains Seraphim Findanides, editor of *Elefterotypia*. 'Northern Europe and America should understand how close we have been to the terrible events happening on our borders, and that we are simply describing them as we see them. Who has a monopoly on truth?'

There were, however, a few dissenting voices. In *To Vima*, respected commentator Dimitris Psychogios railed against the media establishment for 'scaremongering about radioactivity because they are simply trying to take revenge for the defeat of Milosevic, whom they had supported for years.' He charged them with a 'hypocritical pacifism that remained silent during the decade when various Arkan-like heroes were carrying out massacres'. This scaremongering, says Psychogios, is symptomatic of a 'serious malaise' in Greek journalism when it comes to 'national issues'.

Takis Michas, a writer for *Eleutherotypia* and author of the forthcoming book *Unholy Alliance – The Athens–Milosevic Axis 1991–2000*, offers some examples of the way this malaise shaped Greek coverage of the NATO attack on Yugoslavia in 1999. 'The picture of the war emerging from the media was a totally different one from the picture that predominated in the West,' he says. 'It was as if one were dealing with two different wars. The main difference concerned the attribution of blame. All the Greek dailies, without exception, blamed NATO and the US for the outbreak of hostilities. Albanians were generally portrayed as fleeing not because they were being expelled by the Serbs, but because of NATO bombings. The Greek media attributed the mass destruction of property in Kosovo to the NATO bombings; the western media, to burning by the Serbs.' From the first night of hostilities, all the television channels transmitted pictures that purported to portray NATO air attacks against Priština: 'However,' Michas says, 'it is by now established that the first NATO rocket hit Priština a week after the initiation of NATO's air attacks against Yugoslavia.'

As John Carr points out in an elegantly argued dissertation, *Manufacturing the Enemy: Nationalism and Turkophobia in the Greek Media*, the Greek press has been dominated by nationalist ideology since its inception: 'Whereas the western press developed in response to a need for public information on the part of an increasingly articulate and politically conscious, albeit limited, public, the Greek press was from the outset recruited into the process of nationalist myth-making and myth perpetuation.' Veteran journalist Richardo Someritis sums it up succinctly: 'Many Greek journalists behave like soldiers at the front: they have chosen their camp, their uniform, their flag.'

Since the collapse of the Colonels' dictatorship in 1974, freedom of expression has been regarded as sacrosanct and attempts at direct

Opinions for sale. Credit: © Constantine Manos / Magnum

censorship usually meet with uproar. But such is the force of the historically and culturally reinforced us-and-them discourse that stepping out of line is seen as serving foreign, and therefore hostile, interests. In its joint annual report for 1999, Greek Helsinki Monitor and the Minority Rights Group Greece conclude that 'although most journalists would deny its existence, self-censorship, especially on sensitive "national issues", is a common practice among journalists in order to preserve their jobs and status.'

Privately owned media outlets have mushroomed – particularly since 1990, when the government liberalised the airwaves. In a country of just 10 million people, there are some 35 national papers, 10 major TV channels and 2,500 radio stations. Serapheim Findanides says such a broad media scene is 'evidence of a healthy exchange of ideas and information'. But the competition for audience and advertising revenue is intense. Rather than diversity of opinion, there is what one journalist calls a 'diversity of propaganda'. Over the last ten years, newspaper readership has halved as more and more Greeks turn to the television for news. And, as Someritis argues, it is the policy of the channel bosses 'to make the viewer feel threatened'. Fear sells, apparently.

The coverage of the DU affair provides a case study of how this heady – and evidently profitable – mix of nationalism and populism in an ostensibly free press is amplified by the complex, often corrupt, relationship between journalists, editors, media owners, big business and the state – what Greeks call *diaplekomena* (entanglements). There is hardly a media baron who doesn't own other companies – dealing in, for example, construction, arms or communications.

Virginia Tsouderou, president of the Greek branch of Transparency International, is campaigning to bar media owners from bidding for public works contracts. 'Some media owners have created gigantic companies, which are involved in almost all aspects of business,' she says. 'Their influence upon politicians becomes enormous due to the fact that they own national broadcasting [and recently local] TV and radio stations and newspapers. In practice, they can blackmail MPs by blacklisting them and excluding them from their TV and radio channels.' It is not difficult to see how this undermines the media's ability to monitor government malpractice and corruption, or take an independent line on national issues.

Greece's only media watchdog is the lame National Radio and Television Council (NRTC). Set up in 1989, the council includes representatives from all political parties, but has been largely ignored. The NRTC's remit, among other things, is to discourage 'racism and xenophobia' in news and current affairs. It is currently wrestling with the *diaplekomena* issue, trying to set limits on cross-media ownership. Critics say, however, that until the NRTC is free of political influence, little can be expected of it.

Someritis believes that the journalists' union should clean its own house. 'Shouldn't it remind journalists that their role is to inform? I wonder if our statutes and code of ethics have been replaced by declarations of various committees of "friendship" and propaganda.'

This is not to suggest that audiences soak up the nationalism and myth-making like a sponge. In a recent survey of Greeks' faith in their institutions, only the Church and the military garnered a majority. The media came way down the list, just ahead of the country's politicians but behind its courts. One 'dissident' was branded an 'anti-clerical traitor' for pointing out that 'if the Church and the military are the institutions Greeks trust most, the country is in deep trouble'. ❑

Michael Howard is editor of Odyssey magazine in Athens, a founding editor of Cairo Times and a contributor to the Guardian

GAZMEND KAPLLANI

Walking down Mitropoleos Street

Before 1991 there was a very short joke making the rounds in Greece: 'Albanian tourist'

In 1991, when Albania's communist government collapsed, an exodus began towards 'the West'. Ten years later, 800,000 Albanians, mostly young people, have abandoned their country of 3.5 million and scattered to the four winds. The greatest numbers are in Albania's neighbouring countries, Italy and Greece. They work in factories, on building sites, as petrol pump attendants, pizza-delivery men, waiters, cleaners, shepherds and farm labourers.

A few decades ago, Greece was a country of mass emigration. Between 1960 and 1975, 800,000 Greeks passed through the factories of Germany. Since 1991, according to the best estimates, 500,000 to 600,000 immigrants have arrived in Greece (population 9 million), more than 60 per cent of them from Albania.

Until the beginning of 1998, the hundreds of thousands of immigrants existed *de facto* but not *de jure*. Then came the official recognition that Greece had become a country of immigration. A Green Card law was passed, administered by the Ministry of Labour and Social Security, to 'restore' order to the labour market after eight years of chaos. The results have been mixed, to say the least. According to the pro-government newspaper *Ta Nea*, by the summer of 2000 only 225,691 aliens had applied for the card and fewer than 120,000 had succeeded despite passing through 'an incredible ordeal'.

In the meantime, 'the Albanian' has become the villain of the small screen, the media's favourite scapegoat for every social ill. A recent survey found that the Albanians' bad image among parents, teachers and schoolchildren rivalled even that of the Turks. But while the Turks are 'over there', the Albanians are over here, sharing classrooms with those same children.

Helidon Haliti is a painter, a graduate of Albania's School of Fine Arts.

'I came to Greece in 1992, uninvited and illegal. I paid a taxi driver 60,000 drachmas (US$162) and he brought me to Athens. At first I felt lost in this city: its size frightened me. I did casual labour so that I could survive. My first "real" job was in a cemetery, decorating the dead with flowers. Gradually I found work closer to my interests – commissions for "traditional" paintings. In 1998 I began the process of becoming legal. Being illegal is a torment I wouldn't wish on my worst enemy. It's terrible, the feeling that you exist but, at the same time, don't exist. When you're illegal you try to become as invisible as possible – invisible to police checks. And when the press carries stories week after week about the "bad Albanians" who have "invaded" Greece, you try to become even more invisible.

'I came to stay for a few years. I work a lot. I survive and I try to paint. A few weeks ago, after many difficulties, we put on a show of paintings in a gallery with some other Albanian artists – also immigrants – which got a very good response. It was the first time I'd seen my work under my own signature, my real name. My employers encourage me always to sign my name in Greek and to introduce myself not as an Albanian but as a Northern Epirote [the name given in Greece to the Greek minority in southern Albania]. Nationality is stronger than art, in other words.

'I don't think of the future much because it makes me anxious. When I do think of it, I always insist that I'll go back to Albania. That's what I used to say at the beginning, too: three years and then I'll go back. And it has been nearly ten. Leaving home is a great trap. Now I have a two-month-old daughter. I'm starting to like this city, this life. The future? I don't know.'

Nevruzete G is 45 years old. She lost everything she had in the infamous pyramid schemes and crossed illegally into Greece with her family in 1997. She found a job and a home. When the Green Card law was passed, she rushed to get her papers in order. On 14 May 2000 she went to Albania for three days. On her return, the Greek policeman checking passports said her passport was forged and denied her entry, saying she needed a visa.

'I sent the passport to my husband in Athens to find a lawyer to show that it wasn't forged. A month went by. I had to get back as soon as possible so as not to lose my job. I got another passport. I queued at the embassy for a visa. I went in three times and they denied me the visa. The fourth time I paid a go-between – someone my neighbour knew – 400,000 drachmas (US$1,080). After that I went to the embassy and got the visa with no problem. I set out the same day and crossed the border.

'This all took two months, and, when I got back to Athens, I discovered I had lost my job. After two and a half months, I got confirmation from the ministry of public order that my passport was not forged. After three months I got my papers back. That wasn't all. After two weeks, "Operation Broom" picked up my 15-year-old son Ervis. Though he had the necessary papers, the police deported him. Two months later, with the intervention of Greek Helsinki Watch and the Citizens' Ombudsman, the police accepted their mistake and gave the order for my child to come back. After that I'm afraid to go to Albania in case the officer at the border makes another "mistake". I've told my son not to go out too much.'

Arban Perlala, 17, came to Greece with his parents for an eye operation six years ago. Arban and his parents will never forget the affection and support offered them by ordinary people whom they met in Greece. Because the treatment took a long time, and because life in Albania was very hard, the family decided to stay as illegal immigrants. Arban entered a Greek school, made friends, became interested in computers and rap music, and life went on. Until 15 January 1999, when he was arrested and charged with throwing a Molotov cocktail at a riot policeman during a demonstration against the government's education reforms. In spite of the testimony of his teachers, fellow students and of a well-known journalist – who made a documentary to prove Arban's innocence – he was sentenced to eight and a half years in prison. He is now free, pending appeal.

'On 15 January, at about 10.30 in the morning, 25 or 30 of us set out for the march. When we reached Stadiou Street at noon we met our teacher, Eleni Lapathioti. Kids from my school stayed in sight of each other. In particular, Anna Plaouskou, Evanthia Katsakiori and I stayed together the whole time. When we arrived at Klafthmonos Square the march stopped. We learned from some other students that there had been incidents in Syntagma Square. After a while, the march set off again. When we arrived outside McDonald's we decided to go home because we were all tired. We told our teacher, Mrs Eleni, that we were leaving and set out for the number 25 bus stop in Monastiraki.

'As we were walking down Mitropoleos Street, we found ourselves in the middle of a squad of riot policemen. We were walking normally, with nothing in our hands or pockets except our personal effects, and with the sole aim of reaching the number 25 bus stop. One of the policemen pounced on me, and others followed. During my arrest [at 1.15pm according to videotapes recorded by the Alpha, Antena and Mega TV channels] I put up no resistance – how could I when I was surrounded by policemen kicking me and beating me with heavy objects? I couldn't see the weapons because I had been struck in the left eye – on which I had had the operation – and fainted from physical pain and shock. I assume they were helmets or clubs.

'From then on, the drill was beatings on a daily basis, detention in the cells of the general police headquarters, going back and forth to court, beatings in the court building, insults to my country of origin from every policeman who saw me, remand on serious charges in the judicial prison of Volos, visits to the Prisoners' Hospital in Athens because of my awful state of health, release on bail, court, my conviction on serious charges (which are not true) and my release – free, pending appeal. I am sure that all those who have not hesitated to treat a 17-year-old in such a harsh, violent and inhuman way, just because he is of Albanian origin, will have to account for themselves one day to Him who is my irrefutable witness.' ❏

Gazmend Kapllani is a journalist and writer living in Athens. He can be contacted at shqip@ath.forthnet.gr. If you want to talk to Arban, you can reach him at rrmrap@yahoo.com. Translated by Maria Margaronis

Culture

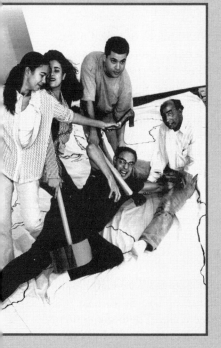

On the set of Aisha and the Women of Medina. *Credit: Maarten Laupman*

EDWARD LUCIE-SMITH

Notes from a censored man

I never think of myself as someone who is going to be – or who is likely to be – censored. Recent experiences have tended to prove me wrong. The sting in these experiences has not been the act of censorship itself, but the identity of the censors. Essentially, they are people who ought to have been on my side of the fence

If, as I did recently, you publish a book of photographs of naked men, sometimes alone, sometimes in couples, you must, I suppose, even today, expect a few people to hold up their hands in horror. The expectation is more likely to be fulfilled if the pictures show, as a number of mine do, men embracing or apparently making love. The book does, however, make a polemical point, or several polemical points. The title is *Flesh and Stone*, and the pictures of living men – warm, breathing flesh – are interspersed with pictures of statues and sculptural groups, ranging in date from antiquity to the mid-twentieth century. The pictures are taken in such a way that the viewer can't always immediately tell what is flesh and what is stone. In fact, it sometimes seems as if the sculptures show men committing sexual acts. The point here is that when we look at famous sculptures in museums or in public places we somehow assume that all the messages they have for us are innocent. If we care to look more closely, that isn't the case at all.

Another theme in the book is the frantic efforts made by eighteenth- and nineteenth-century sculptors in particular to present nude male figures while still somehow concealing their genitalia. The book contains some pictures illustrating the more unlikely devices used – devices that often simply call attention to the body parts they are meant to conceal.

It also features, not just a suite of pictures, but a long essay that considers all the issues involved in photographing the nude male. The essay makes it quite clear that the pictures have a serious point, and raise substantial issues about current attitudes to the male body and to erotic representations in general. It continues a discourse which features in a number of other books I have published.

One might assume that such a book would be of great interest to the large American gay community – but one publication that declared it was too hot for them to handle was the American publication *The Advocate*, a broadsheet that is usually viewed as the journal of record for gays in the United States. The refusal extended not only to featuring the book, but to reviewing it. Protesting that she nevertheless 'had the greatest respect' for me and my work, *The Advocate* spokesperson explained that the book 'was too hot for us to handle'. This attitude can be considered odd on quite a number of grounds. The first is that *The Advocate* issues an advertising supplement (subscribers only) in which you can find not only fairly explicit contact ads but advertisements for every kind of sex aid and for the services of male prostitutes – call them 'escorts' if you prefer. The second is that *The Advocate* used to have a sister publication called *Advocate Men*, a colour magazine largely devoted to pictures of muscular young men in the nude, quite often with erections. This publication still exists, but is now called simply *Men* – a change that is significant in itself. You can still buy *Advocate Men* videos on the Web, in which models who have appeared in the magazine strip off and masturbate for the delectation of the viewer.

What is going on?

The answer lies in the present condition of US society. Even before the election of George W Bush to the presidency, *The Advocate* was running scared. Its pages are full of articles about why a Republican government is going to be a bad thing for homosexuals, gay men in particular. Rather than fight, the paper has decided to keep its head down. Despite its proud title, certain kinds of advocacy now seem too much of a risk. Does this seem a familiar kind of cut-and-run? I'm afraid it does. The lessons offered by history, especially those of the first half of the twentieth century, are being forgotten in the US.

They are also being forgotten here in Britain. The last book of mine which I would ever expect to run into a censorship problem is *Movements in Modern Art*. In various forms, this has been continuously in

EDWARD LUCIE-SMITH

print since 1969. Recently, the publisher, Thames & Hudson, asked me
to prepare a radically revised new addition. One of the developments
I wanted to take into account was what was happening in Russia.
A group of artists in St Petersburg called the Novia Akademia now
seek to combine what they see as 'classical values' with modern digital
techniques. One of the most prominent artists in the group is Olga
Tobreluts. One of the things Tobreluts has become famous for is melding
Old Master paintings with the faces of modern celebrities – a digital
development of photomontage. One of her most celebrated images
shows a Perugino St Sebastian with the features of the film star
Leonardo DiCaprio. The image was included in the 'Heaven'
exhibition, originated by the Kunsthalle Düsseldorf and later seen at
the Tate Gallery, Liverpool. If memory serves, it was illustrated in a
review of the show published in *The Times* (15 December 1999). The
catalogue, published by Hatje Kantz Verlag and freely available in the
US in its English-text version, also illustrates the image.

No problem in using this, one might have thought. But no: Thames
& Hudson's lawyers took fright because the book was being published
not only here but in the US, where celebrities patent their images and
are sometimes ferocious in defending them. 'You can't use that,' I was
told, 'the risk is too great.' Let us once again turn to history. In the
1930s, John Heartfield used a cruder version of the techniques Tobreluts
now employs to create ferocious attacks on the Nazi leadership. Suppose
Hitler or Goebbels or Goering had been able to patent their images in
the same way. Suppose, even, that one of them was still alive and living
in the US. Would Thames & Hudson dare to publish the picture? Given
my recent experience, probably not.

I am left with two rueful reflections. One is that Thames & Hudson
was founded by a refugee from Nazism, Walter Neurath. It was he who
commissioned *Movements in Modern Art*, shortly before his death. The
other is that if George W Bush takes the same precautions as the likes of
Leonardo DiCaprio, nobody – not *The Advocate*, not even the *New York
Times* – can safely publish a photomontage satirising him. And probably
not even a caricature in which he is fully recognisable. We live in
interesting times. ❏

Edward Lucie-Smith *is a writer and art critic. His most recent book,* Flesh and
Stone, *was published last year by Ipso Facto*

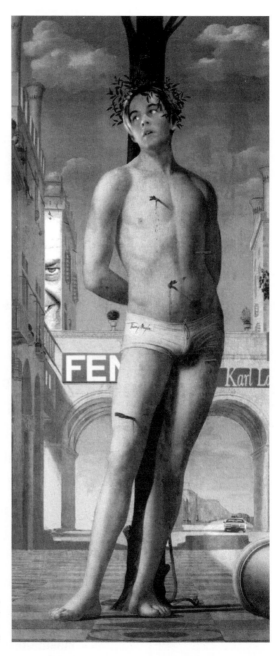

Leonardo DiCaprio
by Olga Tobreluts:
playing with Perugino.
Credit: Art Kiosk Belgium

WIJBRAND SCHAAP

Aisha in trouble

**The long arm of intimidation reached deep into Rotterdam
last year to silence the tale of one of Islam's most astonishing
women**

'Suddenly our beards started growing,' joked a man from Rotterdam's
Society for Young Arabs (SAJ) when asked about the organisation's
role in the cancellation of the opera *Aisha and the Women of Medina*.
'We're not fundamentalists. The SAJ is a liberal, if not a left-wing
organisation. Some of our members are political refugees. But we
were concerned about possible negative reactions among the Moroccan
community in Rotterdam. We asked for caution.'

The SAJ's name came up last November when one of The
Netherlands' best independent theatre companies, Het Onafhankelijk
Toneel (OT), cancelled the production of an opera based on Assia
Djebar's novel *Far from Medina*, two weeks before the start of rehearsals.
The Moroccan actors, singers, the composer and even some of the
musicians refused to participate when a fax was sent to a Moroccan
newspaper and the ministry of the interior, denouncing them for
being involved in a work that would offend the Prophet Mohammed
and 'degrade him as a pederast'. According to the fax, the physical
representation of Aisha, youngest wife of the Prophet, is also forbidden.

OT's artistic director, Gerrit Timmers, said: 'I'm stunned. We
contracted the actors and musicians in June. They knew the opera
would be about Aisha and that she would appear on stage. They didn't
object then. They were given the French script in July. They agreed
to perform. It's strange that only now they suddenly back out.'

Assia Djebar's opera focuses on the relationship between the Prophet
and his youngest wife, whom he married when she was nine. According
to Djebar, her youth gave Aisha a chance to view her husband's life
with more detachment, while more than 2,000 *hadiths* (religious

O.T. SPEELT — AÏSJA EN DE VROUWEN VAN MEDINA

statements) were once attributed to her. Djebar's opera deals with events surrounding Aisha's disappearance in the desert, from where she is rescued by one of the Prophet's followers. She was subsequently accused of adultery, and her trial led to one of the most important marriage laws in Islam. To prove his wife's adultery, a husband must find four independent witnesses.

Mohammed is not shown on stage in the opera and nor is his closest companion, Abu Bakr. He is quoted, however, though only in the way he is quoted by early Islamic historians: 'The Prophet says . . .' There was genuine concern that the Prophet would emerge from the opera as a pederast, but Timmers denies this. 'We have carefully left out any – however historically correct – allusion to eroticism between the old man and the young girl. But the Prophet is characterised as a human being, the way he demanded to be seen by his followers.'

Saïda Baadi, a Moroccan actress who was to have played a major role, claims ignorance. 'I've worked with Gerrit Timmers before and I know him to be very cautious. I may be naive, but I didn't know it was forbidden to show Aisha on stage. It was only when we received a phone call from people of the socialist party that we found out we were about to embark on a dangerous project.' Not only was the staging of Aisha 'wrong', but also the way the Prophet was portrayed. 'Only when we got the definitive text in classical Arabic could we see that He could be interpreted as having been a pederast. That would have been a disaster. I still want to live and work in Morocco. We told Gerrit it was too dangerous. We could do a version in which Aisha was invisible to the audience.'

This was unacceptable. 'It would be like playing *Hamlet* without Hamlet. There would be nothing left.' Najib Cherradi, composer of the music for *Aisha*, and Mohammed Khnous, one of the musicians, decided to take the matter to court for Dfl 53,000 (US$22,250) in lost earnings, claiming Timmers could easily have put Aisha behind a curtain. The Dutch court ruled against them.

After a protracted government silence over what has come to be known as the 'Aisha Affair', Culture Minister Rick van der Ploeg admitted in January that the case was under investigation by its Foreign Intelligence Service, the BVD, and there had been top-level

Flyer advertising Aisha and the Women of Medina. *Credit: OT*

communications with the Moroccan government. Officially, there is no religious objection to putting Aisha on stage: another version of the opera, performed by Italian actors, is successfully touring Italy without angering Muslims. In a further twist, the tell-tale fax that started off the whole affair can no longer be traced in the offices to which it was sent in Morocco. The Dutch government can do nothing more: no one can be forced to perform in a play.

The difficulty remains that Gerrit Timmers produces his plays with Moroccan actors and singers. With *Othello*, in which a Dutch general is destroyed by a Moroccan Iago during Operation Desert Storm, and *La Civilisation de ma Mère*, which relates the evolution of an illiterate woman into a fully developed feminist, OT has found a totally new audience in the Moroccan and Arab communities. He doesn't want to lose it. 'If I were to stage this opera with Dutch actors, I would only see Dutch intellectuals in the audience. Everything that I have built up in the last decade would be lost.'

Timmers has not definitely cancelled *Aisha*: 'We are trying to find a way to produce the opera and, at the same time, to prevent any religious fuss. The problem is finding the people in Islam who can give their consent and have sufficient authority to stop any fundamentalist threat from becoming serious. Islam is more anarchist and even more democratic than Christianity. Anyone with a more than average knowledge of the Quran is considered a wise man. So opinions can change, even at Al-Azar University in Cairo. We're trying to find someone who matters. The story of Aisha has to be told. It is not only one of the most beautiful stories I know, it is also one of the most important stories in Islam.' ❏

Wijbrand Schaap is *drama critic at* Algemeen Dagblad *in Rotterdam*

TAOUFIK BEN BRIK

The informer

His column in the tabloid *El Berrah* is unique in Tunisia. Day after day he tracks down information and hunts for a scoop in a country where *omertà* is the rule and where there is a perpetual conspiracy of silence. The first to turn to his column, not always in admiration, it must be said, are those he mentions in his articles. About 4.30 in the afternoon there's a call to extension 666 on the ground floor of the *El Berrah* offices. The voice on the other end sounds like some kind of tough, the kind you might meet in Hay Ettadhamen, a powder-keg area of Tunis. It growls: 'Meet at the Café El Capo in El Manar II. I've got something for you. It's dynamite,' and he hangs up. In the hubbub of the pressroom of the biggest-selling paper in Tunis hardly anyone notices Zine slip out. In the warm November sunshine, outside the République metro station, drivers of yellow cabs hoot and swear in the usual Ramadan traffic jam. Zine gets into his Alfa Romeo and makes his way through the town centre to Manar II to meet his secret informant on the microcosm that is Tunis.

The call came from one of the militants in the Tunisian Human Rights League (LTDH, Ligue tunisienne des droits de l'homme), one of four groups controlling the resistance [Banned again in February. Ed]. His knack of finding such well-placed informants has made Zine, at 63, the best-informed journalist on the Tunisian opposition. Every Thursday he writes his El Kaoued (The Informer) column for *El Berrah*, the only gossip column or rumour mill in the country that deals with the little world of Tunis. It's full of names that seem as if they've come straight out of a list of film credits: Radhia Nassraoui (lawyer to arseholes and desperadoes); Moncef Marzouki (outlaw doctor); Mokhtar Trifi (fugitive president of the LTDH); from exile, of course, Rached Gannouchi (leader of the Islamist movement, Ennahdha); and, from his hiding place, Hamma Hammani (leader of the Tunisian Communist Party, the clandestine POCT). It was thanks to the El Kaoued column that the betrayal of Kamel Ben Hanès became public knowledge. It was this column that revealed why the ruling power had decided to ban the League. This was where news first appeared of secret agreements between the Dakhilia, the ministry of the interior, and certain members of the LTDH, snatches of phone conversations with the 'rights man' that had been recorded by the Istilamet (secret police). Anyone who takes an interest in what's going on in this little world can't afford to miss his column.

'The opposition can't communicate by telephone or send each other faxes, so if they want to know what's afoot they have to read *El Berrah*,' explains Emile Habouba, the author of *El Haoula* (The Nameless Ones), the best account there is of the world of the informant. Every Thursday morning, the Renault 4s, the 'people's cars', stop in front of the newspaper kiosks. You can be sure that Am Ali Ben Salem, a former resistance fighter, or Khemaïs Ksila, a former prisoner of conscience, will get out and say: '*El Berrah, min fadhlek* [please].'

This afternoon, Zine has no idea what his mole is so keen to tell him. His days are made up of a series of secret meetings with police as well as with members of the opposition, and the whole thing makes up a patchwork of rumours and stories about life on the street.

Reporting such tip-offs, *istoufida*, involves certain risks, and Zine makes sure the meeting takes place where there are plenty of people around. Upsetting the opposition could be fatal. A few weeks before, the general secretary of the ruling party, the Rassemblement constitutionnel démocratique (RCD), Abderrahim Zouari, had been strung up in the media. Although journalists have always escaped attack, the climate is beginning to change now that the opposition has suffered a succession of severe blows and several of its leaders are on trial.

Zine parks two blocks away and goes to the café on foot. His contact is already there: a burly man in a brown overcoat who immediately insists they walk to another place. Zine isn't the only one who is afraid of being seen. Members of the opposition traditionally take a vow of silence when they join. But talking to Zine seems to be OK, as long as no one knows you're doing it. After a few pleasantries, the LTDH mole asks:

'Did you know Kamel Ben Hanès has gone over to the other side?'

Zine is flabbergasted. It's a scoop. What he is being told is that Kamel Ben Hanès's defection is going to be a terrible blow to the LTDH.

Kamel Ben Hanès is a man of about 50, small, slight and balding; he looks more like a bank clerk than a journalist. He is known to have contacts in the closed world of the UGTT, the General Workers' Union, the UGET, the General Students' Union, and the ATJA, the Association of Young Lawyers. Zine makes a rapid note of the details of what his informer has to say. Kamel had been an unsuccessful candidate at the last LTDH congress. To get his revenge, he'd lodged an official complaint, calling for the cancellation of the fifth congress. The meeting has taken only a few minutes. It's been a good afternoon's work: another scoop for El Kaoued.

On the streets of Tunis. Credit: © Börje Tobiasson / Panos Pictures

Zine leaves his home in Carthage, a prosperous suburb of Tunis, at 8am, after making a series of routine phone calls to his police contacts. Every morning he calls a dozen or so officials in the state prosecutor's office. Then he goes to the court to watch the trial that is under way. After that, he criss-crosses the town, moving from lawyers' offices to the dodgy bars on Avenue Farhat-Hached and talking to people from the 3Ps – police, party, punks. Covering the activities of this microcosm is an enormous task and it has no boundaries: it stretches into every aspect of the life of the city. Zine is a reporter of the old school, something of a rarity in the world of office-based journalists. In fact, he had never been the slightest bit interested in what was going to happen in the country as a whole or in the big, wide world and only believed, after a fashion, in some sort of hypothetical, distant natural order of things that he couldn't fully grasp. His catalogue of vices is the usual middle-class list: smoking two packs of '20 March' per day (a popular brand of cigarettes in Tunisia, where 20 March 1956 is Independence Day); drinking anything with alcohol in it and, in a rueful sort of way, eyeing up the flocks of suntanned women with improbable breasts who stride insolently and unaccompanied through the streets of Tunis City.

Nothing else interests him. In a way, he sees himself as an outsider among the Tunisians: someone who has lost the ability to be interested in anything at all, even in himself. Perhaps that is why he became a master-informer. In a country where informing is the national sport, Zine's ambition is to be the ultimate champion in every category.

Like all the great predators, Zine is only interested in big game. Like archaeologists of old, he probes into the soul of his target until he finds the opening that leads to the great discovery. He isn't interested in petty betrayals. He is very discreet and, for a man whose revelations make so much noise, he is well camouflaged against the background of Tunis. Above all, he shuns attention.

'It's not something shameful, it's just a job like any other. You just have to enjoy listening in on bits of people's lives. I'm a sort of information exchange.'

More often than not, his victims come along of their own accord to supply him with an item of information to add to his column. Recently, he got a call from an opposition contact in exile telling him that Kamel Jendoubi, an important figure, had cancer. After a day sniffing around, Zine had his exclusive story. Everyone in opposition circles knows him.

Going into the courtroom building with him is like going to a football match with Chokvi el-Ouer, the national team's goalkeeper. With the exception of two or three individuals who cut him dead, people nod to him or say hello. 'Not one of my fan club,' says Zine, pointing out Omar Mestri, a hot-tempered militant who gives him the cold shoulder. Moncef Marzouki, spokesman for the National Council for Civil Liberties (CNLT) in Tunisia, is even less pleased to see him. He is on trial for membership of an unauthorised association, spreading false rumours, slandering the police force and incitement to sedition.

From the dock, Marzouki nudges his lawyer Béchir Essid when he sees Zine slip quietly into the court.

'It's that grass Zine,' mutters Moncef. The magistrate looks up. Zine doesn't react. He's used to that kind of attention and, anyway, he knows that Moncef is likely to spend the rest of his life in prison. The silly sod thought he was going to move into the presidential palace in Carthage! Dream on! For 40 minutes Zine takes notes then quietly leaves the court. He goes to a phone box and calls Taoufik Boûn, head of the presidential police force, to put him in the picture.

In the same court building the trial of a lawyer named Néjib Hosni is in progress. He gets frequent mention in Zine's column. In June 1994, he was arrested and charged with falsification of public accounts in respect of the sale of some pathetic little patch of land. Néjib was sentenced to eight years' imprisonment and forbidden to practise for five years.

The trial has been going on for hours and Zine is the only reporter present. When he enters the courtroom, Néjib scowls at him. Zine takes notes, while the judge delivers the verdict. It's good copy, but there's no chance of a scoop, so Zine leaves. He meets a tax inspector on the stairs and stops to have a chat with him: he knows he might need to call on him some day. After all, when they finally managed to get Ismaïel Sahbani, the otherwise irremovable general secretary of the union, it was for 'embezzlement' of UGTT funds. In fact, Zine has a healthy and equal mistrust of both the cops and members of the opposition; he believes you have to tell both sides of the story. 'Being an informer means profiting from both sides, the victims and the secret police,' he says. ❑

*Back in Tunis after his hunger strike (*Index 1/2001*), writer and journalist* **Taoufik Ben Brik** *has turned to fiction. This story was first published in French in* Le Courrier de Genève. *Translated by Mike Routledge*

Stand

BRITAIN'S FOREMOST LITERARY QUARTERLY

EDITORS

Michael Hulse
John Kinsella

EDITORIAL OFFICE

School of English
University of Leeds
Leeds LS2 9JT
UK
PH: +44 (0) 113 233 4794
FAX: +44 (0) 113 233 4791
EMAIL:
stand@english.novell.leeds.ac.uk
WEBSITE:
http://saturn.vcu.edu/~dlatane/stand.html

SUBSCRIPTIONS

Worldwide Subscriptions
Unit 4, Gibbs Reed Farm
Ticehurst
East Sussex TN5 7HE
UK
PH:+44 (0) 1580 200657
FAX:+44 (0) 1580 200616
EMAIL:wws.subscription@virgin.net

SUBSCRIPTION RATES

One Year: £25.00 (UK and Europe)
(£31.00/US$49.50 overseas)
Student/Unwaged: £18.00
(£19.00/US$30.00)
Single copy (by mail): £7.00
(£8.00/US$13.00)

IN SEPTEMBER 2000

New work from New Zealand writers including Barbara Anderson, Lauris Edmond, Charlotte Grimshaw, Bill Manhire, Vincent O'Sullivan and Elizabeth Smither. Plus poetry by Charles Boyle and Sheenagh Pugh, fiction by Brian Howell, and Glyn Maxwell's *ars poetica*.

DECEMBER 2000/MARCH 2001

DOUBLE NOBEL PRIZE ISSUE

In partnership with *The Kenyon Review*, a major issue celebrating the first century of the Nobel Prize, to mark and accompany the Nobel Museum's exhibition as it begins four years travelling the world.

"IF YOU WANT THE EXCITEMENT OF ORIGINAL LITERARY ACHIEVEMENT, OF A PASSION FOR IT, I RECOMMEND *STAND*."

RICHARD HOLMES

MICHAEL EAUDE

Trip to Collioure

Republican exiles from the Spanish Civil War are still waiting for the return of their citizenship 60 years after their defeat by General Franco's fascist troops

The two coaches are due to leave before dawn from the Plaça de Catalunya, the ugly central square in the middle of fashionable Barcelona. We are off for the day to Collioure, across the border and the mountains into France, at the end of the Second International Congress on the Spanish Literary Exile of 1939.

For five days, we have listened to 20 or so 'testimonies' from Republican exiles, old men and women from Chile, Mexico, France. Franco's victory in 1939 drove into exile the best of Spain's artists, scientists and educators with their liberal and socialist ideas, as well as hundreds of thousands of civilians and fighters. This trip is about memory confronted with oblivion; about Spain's effort to write out of its recent history all those who were driven out of the country by Franco's victory 60 years ago.

The journey up the motorway to the frontier at La Jonquera takes an hour and a half; it evokes memories of the mass exodus after the fall of Barcelona on 25 January 1939 when civilians and the Republican army began massing on this border to escape Franco's armies. As dawn breaks, the snow glinting on the Pyrenees reminds us what it must have been like to walk this 100-mile route in midwinter. The Daladier government which replaced Leon Blum's Popular Front had closed the border. Xenophobia dominated the French press, stirring up public opinion against the wild revolutionaries who were going to invade the country, along with the filthy poor who were going to ravage it with epidemics. As the numbers of civilians sleeping out unprotected from rain and sleet increased, Daladier was finally forced to open the border on the night of 6/7 February.

A few days short of her 34th birthday, Frederica Montseny reached this border with her five-year-old daughter, seven-month-old son and her mother on a stretcher. Her partner, Germinal, was fighting in the rearguard action that held up Franco's troops long enough for the population to reach France. Montseny had been Minister of Health – the first woman and the first anarchist ever to be a minister in Spain – in Largo Caballero's 1936/37 Popular Front Government.

Montseny wrote: 'Women who had spent several nights under the rain with suckling children in their arms filled the dispensary [of the frontier town Le Perthus] and showed their coughing children to Dr Serrano. Completely overwhelmed, Serrano told me in a low voice, "Most of these will die. They've all got pneumonia. If I was able to look after them, some could be saved. But there's nothing we can do, no hospital to take them to . . ."'

The defeated Republicans approached France with a hope: the war might be lost, but they could find refuge and then work for Franco's fall. They had not expected to be greeted like pariahs. It is worth quoting Montseny again; the anger still quivers in her sentences, even though they were written ten years later: 'These mothers and children had spent the night in Le Perthus. No one knew how they had crossed the frontier. They remained the whole night huddled on the pavements, in the doorways of houses where families inside heard from their warm beds how the babies and mothers cried. No door was opened for them. In the harsh darkness of the night, there was only one thing darker and harsher than the night itself: the soul of men.'

After a 30-minute drive, the coach winds down into Collioure, a picture-book village of neat red-roofed houses and tree-filled gardens round a blue bay. Matisse, Dufy and Les Fauves came here in the first years of the century. 'There is no sky in France bluer than that of Collioure . . . I only have to close the shutters to keep in my room all the colours of the Mediterranean,' wrote Matisse. Today we assemble at the railway station in a drizzle. The morning is devoted to following the Antonio Machado route.

On 22 January 1939, Machado, Spain's most famous living poet, arrived here by train from Barcelona, exhausted and accompanied by his octogenarian mother. He died precisely one month later; his mother three days after him. The poet had written that he would die if ever uprooted from his native land. As such, his choice to remain near the border and his death came to represent the anonymous deaths of so many in that exile.

Waiting on the platform I talk to a round-faced old man, his face wrinkled with deep lines of laughter. He lives in Toulouse. 'Have you never wanted to go back to Spain?' I ask. With a tranquil smile, he delivers his devastating lines: 'I crossed the border when I was 18. And I have never been back to Spain. I won't go, because the democracy in Spain has never recognised us exiles.'

The group of academics and exiles is led off by Monique Alonso. Her face, dress and manners are French, but she is Spanish, the daughter of Spanish exiles, speaking fluent Spanish with a French accent. 'I am 60 years old. I too crossed the border that cruel February, but as something between a feeling and a person. I was a foetus in my mother's belly.'

The last stop on the Machado route is the grave with its inscription, Machado's great lines:

> Cuando llegue el día del último viaje
> Y esté al partir la nave que nunca ha de tornar
> Me encontraréis a bordo ligero de equipaje
> Casi desnudo como los hijos del mar.
> [When the day of the final journey comes
> And the ship that never returns is ready to leave
> You will find me on board free of luggage
> Almost naked like the children of the sea.]

For lunch, we take over a restaurant down by the beach; I ask a big, jovial, red-faced old man what his medals are. He bangs the ribbons on his chest. 'The Légion d'Honneur. I was a guerrilla in World War II. I killed my first German when I was 17,' he grins proudly.

We end our visit in the castle that dominates the waterfront, of terrible memory for the tens of thousands who were crammed into the camps along the beaches of this coast. Having opened the border, the French government had no idea what to do with 200,000–300,000 refugees. It was midwinter and the tramontana whipped the sand across the open camps on the beach.

The refugees, disarmed and defeated, had to build their own barracks. Their latrines were holes in the sand by the sea. Despair was the keynote of those who lay in other holes further up the beach. Most were undernourished, exhausted, cold; some had fled from hospitals with wounds untreated. Gangrene was common. No one knows how many died in St Cyprien, Barcarés, Argeles . . . the beach camps that each held tens of thousands.

Eduardo Pons Prades was part of the team attempting to evacuate the 20,000 Republican wounded from Catalonia. In the face of French disbelief, Pons Prades could only cite the Republicans bayonetted in their hospital beds at Toledo, Albacete and other cities when the Francoist forces entered. The French refused to believe it: this had not happened in World War I.

In 1997, Pons Prades wrote: 'Dysentery and pneumonia ravaged the camps . . . One-third of the internees suffered ringworm and scabies, with frequent ulceration of the skin and inflammation of the throat due to the violent storms of sand caused by the wind. Dr d'Harcourt added that mental and nervous disorders were even more serious than the rest of the illnesses.'

Those who protested at the conditions were sent to Collioure castle, run by the French Foreign Legion, where they were subjected to beatings and solitary confinement. The French were terrified of these 'revolutionaries' overrunning the area and the Prefect was invested with wide-ranging powers.

The man with the medals makes a speech in the long, chill main room of the castle. Big, rough, he explains briefly how tens of thousands of armed Spaniards had participated in the French Maquis from the beginning of World War II. As he steps off the stage he raises his hands to the audience, like a celebrity receiving homage. We do not like him for the way he boasted in the restaurant about killing Germans. But I admire him for his evocation of the thousands of armed Spaniards who continued their resistance in occupied France and contributed so decisively to the liberation.

Other speakers refer to their bitterness when the Allies decided not to overthrow Franco in 1944/45. Antonio Rámirez asks: 'Has that wound of bitterness healed?' There is silence in the hall. Then he answers his own question: 'It has for me, but only after the feeling of fraternity gained in fighting together alongside the French people.'

Tens of thousands of refugees were recruited into the French army after September 1939. But many had already returned to Spain, encouraged by the words of Franco's representatives whom the French government brought into the beach camps to entice the refugees.

Without a boat to America, with only the deep blue sea in front of them, they returned to the devil they knew. Typical among them was one quiet, gentle Republican, whose story was told to us by his daughter. His desire was to get back to his village in Aragón in time to plant the crops. He was imprisoned on his return, as were most. Franco's agents visiting the camps had, of course, promised no reprisals.

It is 11pm by the time the coach pulls up again in modern Barcelona. A very different city from that freezing 26 January 1939 when, in the words of Juan Marsé, Barcelona's finest contemporary novelist, 'men of iron, forged in countless battles, cried like children' in their impotence as Franco's troops paraded along the Diagonal, where the middle class jostled with each other to give the best fascist salute, faces wide open in the explosion of relief that they had survived the revolution.

The day has been scented with the bitter sweetness of defeat that the left evokes to comfort itself. It has been a day about history, about seeking state recognition for the Republican exiles in the knowledge that what happened at beautiful, tranquil Collioure has been too easily forgotten, too willingly buried in the sand of the beaches where only 60 years ago people died in holes in the ground. ❑

Michael Eaude is a freelance writer living in Barcelona

ROBERT CAPA

Retreat to Collioure

Near Barcelona, 25 October 1938:
farewell to the volunteers of the International Brigade

All pictures pp186–89 © Robert Capa / Magnum

Transit, January 1939:
refugees in Barcelona
wait for transit out of
the city before its fall

Retreat, 25–27 January 1939:
on the road from Barcelona

OPPOSITE, ABOVE
Flight, 15 January 1939:
on the road to Barcelona

OPPOSITE, BELOW
Refuge, January 1939:
Republican soldiers
escape to France

Defeat, March 1939:
exiled Republicans are escorted
to internment camps on the
beach at Argelès-sur-Mer,
near Collioure, France

SCOTT CAPURRO

Out in Africa

First it was the Holocaust; then Jesus and the Quran. A stand-up comedian discovers the limits of laughter in South Africa

Good stand-up comedy isn't meant for everybody. A provocative comic, one who can change minds and alter perceptions, is excluded from television, so he or she's an artist, and sorry, but art *isn't* universal. Like any expertise, adroit satire is secular at best and elitist. And lonely. Less than one per cent of the population go to live performances, and only a fraction of that tiny number attend comedy. Yet because everyone sees CNN, everyone surfs the Net, and everyone watches US sitcoms, I figured everyone would understand the humour behind Jesus being a gay icon. And everyone does – in San Francisco and London, where I spend most of my stage time.

But thinking that neophyte comedy producers in South Africa, where alternative comedy has existed for maybe five minutes, would respond passively to the haranguing of some out, obnoxious faggot is more than merely sophomoric. It's not even as charming as the idea that laughter breaks down boundaries. It's actually a narcissistic streak that pushes some performers to drag our tired asses to a police state and slap those 'former' fascists in their Aryan faces with our hard comedy cocks.

The flight to Cape Town from San Francisco takes something like 42 weeks, so I missed the opening night speech/warning from a producer of the Cape Town International Comedy Festival. A speech that, when repeated days later by another comic, sounded more like an omen from a creepy cult member than a 'Break a leg!' kind of pre-show rouser. Apparently, the 12 comics present – six from the UK, four from South Africa, one from Australia, and one other American – were told to stay away from the Muslims. 'The Quran', he says, 'isn't a comic book, it's not like the Bible, you can't write show tunes about it, or sell it on a shopping channel.' The previous year, a local comic made a mosque reference, and wound up with three rifles pointed at his head during performance! So back off, clowns, stay away from the mosque.

With all these warnings, the only place I would've wanted to be on opening night was in the face of some Muslim fundamentalist making fun of female circumcision. Unfortunately, I was changing planes somewhere. When I arrived the next night, I barely had time to get on stage to close a two-and-a-half-hour show. I went over time because the audience seemed to be enjoying themselves. Especially when I said: 'Muslims will fuck anything. I mean, a hole's a hole, right? I'm only quoting the Quran when I say that.'

I heard laughter. Maybe it was my ears still ringing from the flight. I heard applause at the end of my set. Maybe it was the sound of rifles being cocked. I was so sleep-deprived, dehydrated and delusional after being at the mercy of Virgin Economy that I stumbled backstage, slipped on a stair and banged my left shoulder, still sure that my set had gone well. I felt like a clumsy comedy god!

Until I saw the faces of the event's producers backstage. They stared at me, the two of them, whose names I couldn't remember, still can't, so let's call them Blond and Brunette, B&B for short. The blond, the pretty one, drove a convertible Volvo, dressed very smartly and spent the majority of his time in the company of men, while having a 'wife' that no one had ever met. His eyes were about to jump out of their sockets: they weren't just bulging, they were leaving his head animatedly. Because, I suppose, he was shocked and angry and they, the eyes, wanted to escape before his entire cranium exploded. He spat out something about me talking about religion in my act, and how uncomfortable I'd made some members of the audience. 'But', I explained drowsily, 'that's exactly the response I hope for. I mean, isn't this an "edgy" show?'

'Sure,' he said, 'it's edgy, we're performing in the edgy theatre.' The 'edgy theatre' was the smaller of the two huge theatres that make up the Baxter Theatre complex, proud home of classical music during apartheid. In the green room, the walls still displayed photos of the nigger-hating beret-wearers from East Germany and Argentina who had graced the Baxter for 30 years, filling white listeners' ears with stoic, stilted staccato. Now, to represent the drastic changes in the South Africa Constitution – if not the consciousness – the Baxter was home to this festival, the big stage saved for 'mainstream' comics. The smaller stage the technical crew persisted in calling the 'edgy' room, as if they could think of no other name for it. That was the platform from which I, a few minutes before, had changed the face of, well, the producers' faces. They'd been happy with the show until I mentioned that Jesus was a vain Capricorn homo.

Their audience was, the Blond spouted, wealthy, conservative suburbanites. Was I aware of that?

'But those are my people!' I exclaimed. 'I'm like their naughty friend.'

Suddenly I felt like a large ruler was about to whack my back. Producers' fists curled, wry smiles remained on their faces. I was clearly being reprimanded. It was like being caught having sex when you're ten. I knew that, in their eyes, what I'd done was wrong, but it didn't *feel* wrong. It felt so good. Someone shifted. Then coughed. I'm sure it was me. I considered tap-dancing, which always wows a crowd, no matter how sinister their mood.

'We've had bomb threats,' I was told. I wasn't sure if that was meant to discourage me.

'But I make fun of everyone,' my voice spoke. I was sleeping. 'Including myself, to balance the whole thing.'

I was trying to explain irony, the cornerstone of contemporary comedy, to people who'd only recently learned to laugh at something other than blackface and drag. I never really defend myself to people in the business, especially not to my bosses who, I realised, B&B sort of were. A London promoter had offered me this job after a nice, ethnic Australian backed out at the last minute. The Londoner convinced B, squared by fax and email, that I'd do just fine, that I'd played all over the world with little 'friction'. B&B had neglected to watch my tape; I don't even think they knew I was gay until I deep-throated the mike during my set.

I felt set up. I wondered why I wasn't back at my hotel hiring a hooker (they are cheap in South Africa). The promoter, a guy who likes my work and felt bad I was being lashed, sat silently, arms crossed, eyes closed, pretending he was back in London with other people who read for pleasure. I was ordered to cut all the religious stuff out of my act. All of it. Even the stuff about face-fucking Jesus. And though it wasn't my favourite joke before I was told to discard it, once told, it became the crux of my act.

I told them, not only will I not cut it out, but I'll show you how it will work. Again. They threatened to turn off my microphone. I got rid

London 2001:
Scott Capurro live.
Credit: © Wilma Goudappel

of the Muslim jokes instead, and toned down Christ. I wanted to fly home, but my ticket was restricted, like the atmosphere. The Blond's tight-lipped demeanour chilled me. He'd pass me in the hallway, right before my set started, and smile contemptuously. My toes curled. I wondered if he'd hired a firing squad, waiting in the audience for me to open my atheist mouth. Once dead, he could claim he'd warned me. And he'd have been right.

But nothing died, including my act. No matter where they moved me in the bill, buffering me with local comics so that my set would disappear into a long evening, the audience responded well night after night. Well enough for me, which meant a few walkouts, but no one got hurt. But I didn't storm, as the producers hoped, though it wouldn't have swayed their opinion, no matter how well I'd done. They were concerned about the bomb threats, or the death threats to me, which I would've had – have before, always will have – to put up with. They wanted the 'edge' to be soft, the festival to be nice and the audience to come back next year.

I felt hostility everywhere, I felt ashamed and I also felt shunned. I wanted to corner the Blond in the 1970s British Home Stores-style lobby and say: 'Don't fly me eight billion miles and then tell me what I can and cannot do.' Instead I drank beer and cruised straight guys in the lobby. Then the Blond cut me from the Sunday show, because it's 'God's day'. I wondered, what the fuck are God's worshippers doing at an 'edgy' comedy show on a Sunday? I tried to talk my way into the show, only because I hate being excluded, though I adore seeming exclusive.

I cornered the Blond. 'You've got an "edgy" show, and you've cut the edgiest comic off the list?'

'Unfortunately, this is not about you, Mr Capurro.' I was Scott when I'd arrived. 'The theatre must close earlier on Sunday. We're under time constraints.'

Then he dashed, with one of the 'straight' comics in front, laughing and wearing sunglasses at night. They flew off like two characters in a Spanish soap opera, leaving me standing near the Baxter, in Cape Town, thousands of miles from home.

Sunday nights are so quiet when there's no show to do. I wondered if one could commit suicide by smoking too much pot. Anything was better than going to a gay bar, the gay scene there is that bad. Not that you'd know it from travel brochures. Cape Town is promoted as an open-minded, friendly city of the future. That might be, if the future is Muslim bombings – over 140 in 2000 – making it one of the most violent per capita cities in the world.

In South Africa, darkie wants whitey out and the Muslims hate everybody. Our driver, a *progressive* Muslim, carried a .9mm. Not a happy place to raise a minority family, but a fertile ground in which to plant and grow political comedy material. And the local comics, with 'zany' names that sounded like children's candy, and loose ties and perpetual hangovers, mopped the floor with us foreigners. I found them amusing, but the screaming and sweating and 1970s dress code that went along with it were distracting. As were the queer jokes. All four South Africans had queer jokes. Or five of them, actually: the foreigners weren't pulling their weight, so another local male was added to the 'edgy' line-up.

Usually I'd seduce the local comics back at my hotel, but their queer-hating material stifled my erection. And my memory. Because somehow, after that first Sunday, all the religious stuff was back in my act, louder than before. I figured, if they're gonna make fun of fags, then why isn't this OK? Why does censorship start and end with me? ❑

Scott Capurro is a San Francisco-based stand-up whose performance at the Edinburgh Fringe last August ended in uproar after he 'made jokes' about the Holocaust (Index 6/00). His book, Fowl Play, *is published by Headline*